DATE DUE

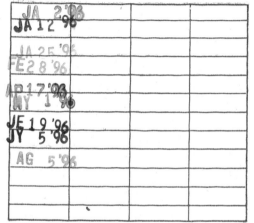

JA 2'96		
JA 12'96		
JA 25'96		
FE 28'96		
AP 17'96		
MY 1'96		
JE 19'96		
JY 5'96		
AG 5'96		

Portraits
of Sarajevo

Portraits
of Sarajevo

Zlatko Dizdarević

Translated by Midhat Ridjanović

Edited by Ammiel Alcalay

FROMM INTERNATIONAL
PUBLISHING CORPORATION
NEW YORK

Manufactured in the United States of America.
Printed on acid-free, recycled paper.
First U.S. edition.

Library of Congress Cataloging-in-Publication Data

Dizdarević, Zlatko.
      [Portraits de Sarajevo. English]
      Portraits of Sarajevo / Zlatko Dizdarević ; translated by Midhat Ridjanović ; edited by Ammiel Alcalay.
            p.   cm.
      Never published in its original Serbo-Croatian (roman) language.
      ISBN 0-88064-167-3 (alk. recycled paper) : $19.95
      1. Sarajevo (Bosnia and Herzegovina—History—Siege, 1992–
      I. Ridjanović, Midhat.   II. Title.
      DR1313.32.S27D613   1995
      949.7'42—dc20   94-43620
                                                          CIP

For Ognjen, Dražen, and Biljana

Introduction

One day, when all of this is over, when the shame of this world is forgotten, when the taste of the defeat and the glory of victory is gone, History will no doubt be enriched with one great name: Sarajevo. And it matters little whether or not that name, and that symbol, will give rise to controversy. "Sarajevo will always be, and everything else will pass," says a song that will live forever. Along with the memory of Sarajevo, a great injustice will be added to history. In fact, it is not the people of Sarajevo that will be remembered, but their city as an idea and as a fact. That is part of the general injustice of this war, which was not waged against cities, or against states, or against nations and borders, but above all and solely against people in the most beautiful sense of that word. If, after what has happened, there can still be a "beautiful sense" of that word.

Of course, no book has ever been able to redress a single historical injustice. Neither will this one. It wasn't meant to in the first place. Nevertheless, it is a small, personal effort so people don't forget Sarajevo and what it was. It aims to bring the story of Sarajevo to the point where it was conceived and where it will end. To try—without being pretentious—to salvage, from under the often artificially constructed and maintained myth about the city, the People of Sarajevo, those that never wanted to be mythologized or immortalized. Those that only wished to remain normal, people going about their business, in their own city, people whose simple wish wasn't granted. Those that never, not even at the end, managed to understand ordinary and simple things and kept asking questions like "Why are they doing it to us?" The last people on this planet to understand that life and death are not controlled by the heart and reason, kindness and happiness, but machinations and greed, force and barbarity.

The people in this book are neither better nor worse than any other Sarajevans. They have not been specially selected, because selection in Sarajevo—at least with regard to the most important matters—stopped when the killing started. They are here because they happened to find themselves along the chronicler's path, just as they might have happened to be in places from which there is no return. Just like that—as they say in Sarajevo.

Time will tell whether it was their luck or their misfortune to have been called by this common name: Sarajevans. As far as the author of this book is concerned, there has, in spite of everything, never been any doubt about it. In the midst of this war, everything has been taken from us except for the fact that we remain Sarajevans, in every sense of that incredible word. In this destitution, we feel a sense of marvel.

> Zlatko Dizdarević
> Sarajevo, March 1994
> (the day after we defeated the
> UNPROFOR soccer team 4 to 0)

Portraits
of Sarajevo

The Bullet and Love

"... I was walking down the street, across Dobrinja, when I was hit by a sniper. Here, see where the bullet went into my head on one side and came out the other. I thought I was done for, but I wasn't. They took me to the hospital, patched me up, and I came out alive. The most important thing is I pulled through. After a month I was up and at 'em, alive and kicking. No kidding, I was perfectly normal, with my head screwed on right. But then I met her, the little fourteen-year-old. And you know what, man? I went completely nuts. In love. Totally nuts. I mean, what the fuck, if you go crazy what can you do. After that the bullet was a piece of cake . . ."

Sixteen-year-old boy from Dobrinja, Sarajevo

Over the Roofs, to the Children

In the second spring of the war, after two years of total darkness, light suddenly came on in the house of the architect Željko Petrović. Without rhyme or reason, contrary to any "logic" of Sarajevo, any "schedule" of power rationing. It was a mystery even for our connoisseurs—specialists at diverting electricity from the main lines that serviced the hospitals, the bakery, or the Post Office. Yet, the story is quite simple.

Željko's kids had been with their mother living as refugees somewhere out there in the big world ever since the beginning of the war. He hadn't been able to speak to them once by phone. For a long time he didn't even know exactly where they were, who they were staying with, or what they lived on. Then, one day, God knows through what channel and whose kindness, Željko found himself with a videotape in his hands, showing his daughter and his son talking about themselves and their mother, pointing at their new teeth that had grown in the meantime, laughing and singing, blowing kisses to their dad and promising him that they would walk around the streets of Sarajevo together and go for trips to the sea again, just like they used to. . . .

So, the tape was in his hands, he knew who sent it and what was on it, but he couldn't see it. There was no electricity. Those who had some remaining car batteries jealously hoarded their "gold reserves" for the latest news about great "diplomatic initiatives," "air strikes," and other such absurdities. Running a VCR and a TV for a full hour takes a lot of juice. Then Željko, having carried the tape around town frantically for three days, came up with an ingenious solution. Some-

2

how, he got a hold of three hundred meters of cable; one night he broke into a small transformer that carried the priority line for the hospital, hooked up his own cable and ran the juice back to his house. That "simple" story went like this:

"An old friend of mine who happens to be an electrical engineer told me how it's done. I didn't dare tell him why I wanted to do it because I was afraid he wouldn't help me if he found out. Of course I had no idea what I was doing and I could have electrocuted myself easily. But that was the furthest thing from my mind. As it was, I would have died carrying around the pictures and voices of my kids without being able to see them. My heart would simply have broken. You should have seen me run that cable. I went along the rooftops, at night, at least where I could get through. Where I couldn't, I knocked on doors of people's apartments and asked them to let me lay the cable through their kitchens, bedrooms, and bathrooms. I told everybody why I was doing it and they all wanted to help. The night we did it, there must have been about twenty people walking around on their roofs, calling out to each other and pulling the cable from house to house. Even the policemen in a guardhouse that we had to cross over pretended not to see or hear anything when I told them what it was all about. I promised them I would steal the electricity for only twenty-four hours and then unhook my cable. They told me not to tell anybody since it might become "contagious." That's how it was. The next day a guy from the electric company that my neighbor brought over checked the work out and said my cable could stay hooked up for another day or two. After that we all watched the tape for the umpteenth time. Even some of my neighbors were crying. . . ."

The rest of the war for the architect Željko Petrović was quite different. Somehow it just become an ordinary war.

On the Road to Ilidža

On Skerlićeva Street, in the center of Sarajevo, a father and his twelve-year-old daughter live. Kasim and Amra. The mother and Amra's brother managed to get out of the city on one of the convoys right at the beginning of the war; they were taken to the Adriatic coast first, then to a village in the Czech Republic, then some relatives in Germany, and finally, through various connections, to Canada. The mother and the son kept hoping that Kasim and Amra would join them, that they would come out of Sarajevo and all start a new life somewhere. But there was no way for a new life to be lived together. A new life did start, but with the family split in half. The hope for imminent change kept dwindling, and life had to be lived. One had to adapt to reality. As a soldier, Kasim spent two days on the front line, mostly at Žuč where it was tougher than anywhere else, and two days at home with his daughter. For two days Amra was on her own, tended to by the neighbors, then the next two days she was with her dad. She lived through the first two days for the sake of the next two. I often see them through my window walking downhill holding hands and carrying a water canister, or going out to what used to be a park to pick up a few remaining twigs to start a fire, or—when the shooting lets up—just going for a walk up and down the street. As winter came with its cold weather, they could no longer be seen out on the street. It seemed, anyway, that I had been seeing less and less of them. Then, one day, as he was coming back from the "line," Kasim came up to me, beaming: "I have to hurry home, Amra is waiting for me so we can go out to Ilidža." For a second I thought I hadn't quite gotten what he said. I

4

thought for a moment that I had misunderstood him. How could he say Ilidža? Ilidža is held by "them," it is beyond the magic line marking free Sarajevo. And, anyway, what business do they have in Ilidža even if they *could* get there?!

"We go by bike. We just enjoy a nice two-hour ride going there and coming back, we meet a lot of people, and we listen to a lot of music. We listen to the news too. . . ." Kasim was telling me this in a kind of conspiratorial tone, obviously relishing my utter perplexity. Then he told me the whole story:

"Before the war my Amra and me, together with Mom and our younger son, used to go to Ilidža on Saturday or Sunday. We'd mount the bikes on the car and just ride around Ilidža all day. Once, a little before the war, Amra tried to persuade me that the two of us— because her brother was too small—should get on our bikes here, in the city, and ride the ten or so kilometers to Ilidža. There and back. I really don't know why, but we somehow let three or four weeks go by without doing it, and then the war came. Amra often reproached me for it, you know how kids do that. The bike trip to Ilidža became like freedom to us, the day of peace, when everything would be the way it was again. We vowed to each other that we would celebrate liberation just like that—by biking out to Ilidža.

"But we made the trip a lot sooner than we'd thought. In fact, we go there now every time I come back from the front line. I hooked up some little gadgets that I concocted myself—onto our bikes—they generate electricity as you pedal. On my bike, we get power for the big radio, and on Amra's for her Walkman. Of course we never agree what to listen to, so she "plugs" her ears with her earphones and listens to music, while I, like all the other idiots around here, listen to the news from dawn to dark, waiting for something that will never come. Pedaling with her hands one day, Amra said to me: 'Listen, Daddy, why couldn't we go to Ilidža with these bikes of ours, like we planned. There, just imagine we got out into the street and started down Njegoševa . . .'

"And that's what happened. We came down Njegoševa Street, turned downhill onto King Tomislav, and then along Tito Street toward Ilidža. On the way we talk about what we see. First, the holes from the shelling on the Bosnian Presidency Building, then the new graves at Ali Pasha's mosque, then the burnt buildings of the Bosnian government and the National Assembly, the National Museum and the one next to it, the Museum of the Revolution, all shut up. Amra always asks me what the Museum of the Revolution is called now, because the new authorities don't like that other revolution and they've taken down signs on streets named after national heroes from the Second World War. And so, on we ride toward Ilidža. We always get upset when we see the hundreds of destroyed houses. On the way, we just have to stop at the big intersections because the traffic lights have all been fixed and so have the trollies. These things, Amra says, were fixed by UNPROFOR. There aren't too many cars so it's easy to ride our bikes. As we speed up past the Television Building, the radio becomes louder and we can't talk, so we slow down.

"And so, to Ilidža. And back. We realized we needed more than two hours. When we 'come home' we're dead but happy as hell. Every time we notice that something has been fixed, or that somebody has begun to fix something. The flower shop by the Insurance Building has started working, and the barricades at the Brotherhood-and-Unity Bridge are gone. Last time Amra noticed that the Megi kiosk at Marindvor, which sold the best and sweetest jelly donuts in town, is going up again. There we had a real problem. I promised her we'd stop at Megi's on the way back and buy some donuts. . . ."

As he was telling me this story, Kasim pointed, joining me in the conspiracy, at a bundle under his arm. "Here are two donuts that Vojo, the cook in my unit at the front line, made for me. He said he was sorry they weren't as good as those at Megi's before the war, but

I'm sure Amra will like these better. The main thing is to keep my promise."

After that, whenever Kasim is home and I see him out in the street with Amra, I know that "they have gone to Ilidža. And I somehow feel good guessing where they are at the moment. Still on Tito Street, or already further out, by the *Oslobodenje* building.

Naive or Stupid

"That fifth of April, 1992, I was standing, together with my colleague Dubravko Brigić, in front of the Bosnian National Assembly building and, in fact, I was doing a live broadcast of the beginning of the war. I had a good view of everything and was watching it with my eyes *and* with the camera. The bullets were whizzing over our heads, I saw the first blood being spilled, the beginning of the destruction. The jet planes of the Yugoslav People's Army pierced the sky above us. On the Vrbanja Bridge, right behind the Assembly building, I see Suada, a college student get killed and I repeat to myself that there is no war, no war. The most incredible thing was that I described everything I saw into the microphone, I kept saying out loud that it was a war, I shouted and cursed, but then again I was saying to myself that it was just a horrible dream, that Sarajevo would continue to live as it always had come tomorrow.

"Just two weeks before that I saw my daughter and grandson off: they were leaving 'for a few days, until the trouble is over.' Two years have gone by and I haven't seen them since. Not once. I haven't heard from them for over a year. Today I'm just happy to know they're safe and sound.

"What came over me and the rest of us on April 5? Why couldn't we see what was right in front of our very noses? I really don't know if we were naive, stupid, or both. My eyes began to open only after that horrendous massacre at the bakery. . . ."

These are the words of Mladen Paunović, a typical representative of the spirit of Sarajevo, maybe also of Sarajevan "stupidity" and stubbornness. Dead serious when he is talking about other people's heroic acts, and always naively laughing when talking about himself. Since his first wound in the leg in July 1992, from a sniper bullet that got him as he was going to the TV station, he has been cracking jokes at his own expense. He would say being shot was naive too. But it wasn't naive at all. After a second wound from shrapnel in the left shoulder in early 1993, he laughed a little less. And, as he put it, "his eyes began to open a little more." In the hospital he met dozens of boys and girls who enthusiastically went to the front to defend their city during the first chaotic days, those who took only their ideals to war and abandoned everything else. Not a single one of them harbored a shred of hatred for anybody, in spite of the fact that they were invalids, that perhaps they would not only never run again, but not even walk.

"I cried for the first time in this war as I was leaving the hospital. It was snowing and, step by step, I was walking downhill. My arm in a metal brace. Four old men made way for me, and one of them, bowing a little, said: 'My respects!'

"That same day at Pofalići, near the tobacco factory, I was watching a man who was hit by a sniper bullet. From time to time he would raise his head slowly as if to plead for help with a fading look of desperation in his eyes. Nobody dared come up to him because the sniper controlled the whole area around the victim. Then, tearing frantically out of nowhere, a beat-up black Audi 80 comes to a screeching halt next to the wounded man, two hands come out of the car and drag him in, and the Audi, with a door dangling open, races off at full speed behind the nearest house, to a shelter, and from there on to the hospital. All of us who watched this from behind a corner knew that it was Mile Plakalović, the taxi driver who spent his whole time saving Sarajevans he didn't even know, taking food for them to the hospital, caring for them. 'Mile the Serb' against the 'so-called Serbs on the hills,' as he himself started calling them. There, I cried twice that day. And I didn't feel bad. I am no hero. Maybe I'm not a coward either, but I'm not too brave. Just so-so. Here, in all this chaos, bravery isn't the point, it's just doing the right thing, honestly and for the sake of doing it. That's why I stayed here, that's why I'll stay to the end. Let everybody who wants out go. The true Sarajevans will stay. Sarajevo is people, real people, and there will never be a shortage of them here.

"By the way, when are you coming back? Isn't it true you won't stay out long? Come on, old buddy, it'll be great again. . . ."

I left him at Aša's, at the Indi. He was drinking some home-made brandy and sharing a good laugh with Aša, as in the happiest of times. Under his arm he was holding a small package of coffee and a few lumps of sugar. An old lady had given it to him in the street, just for the hell of it. She said "Come on, Mladen, my son, take it, please. It's from my son, Sejo. . . ."

The Fountain

"I simply can't forget about that fountain, even now, in the middle of the war. God, how nice it would be, a fountain in front of the cathedral in Sarajevo. Right there, and nowhere else. Why? How should I know why? It all started a long time ago, when I was in Rome and saw one of those beautiful fountains in a square. There were lights under the water, and at night, the jets of water reflected nine different colors. There were figurines made of water that must have been shaped by some kind of pump or machine, it all looked like something out of a fairy tale. I used to go to that fountain every evening; I'd just sit there quietly, smoking, and admiring it. I would smoke in silence and admire it. Sometimes I spent hours there, just sitting and watching it. That's how I decided to build a fountain exactly like that one here in Sarajevo, in front of the cathedral. The Church authorities gave me permission to do it, but not the City. God knows why. I told them everything, that I would go to Rome and find the designer, bring him to Sarajevo, and pay him to build everything that needs to be built. Again they said no. Afterwards they asked me to make a donation for a public tap near the Vijećnica, by some new gas station. You wanted a fountain, they said, fine, now you can have one. We have the design and everything, all you have to do is pay for it. What do I care about your chintzy taps, I told them, I want a fountain like the one in Rome, in front of the cathedral. And you know what, sooner or later, I'm going to build it. Damn right I will, no ifs, ands or buts. I don't care how much it'll cost . . . it's my dream, and the longer this war goes on the more I want to do it. . . ."

Abdulah Hrasnica, businessman

The Meeting

Almost a year after the beginning of the war, I met Babo Tanović on the street. A filmmaker and writer, he's a real man-about-town. He is also known for his appetite and fine feasts. His friends hailed him as one of the greatest connoisseurs of meat and everything possible that can be made from meat. Now, when everyone had already lost a lot of weight, Babo looked just the way he used to in the best of times.

"You really look good, Babo. How do you manage? You must be rolling in dough to be able to pay eighty marks for a kilo of meat."

"True," he said, "it's true that I've got everything I need. . . ."

"Are you serious?"

"Well, in a way, but not the way you think. You know, right after it started, as early as May, I realized what was going on, where it was taking us and the fine times we could look forward to. No one really believed me, but I knew. Then, one fine day I called a meeting with myself. I said to myself: 'Listen, Babo, we've both had it. No money, no meat, no cheese, no wine, no hors d'oeuvres. No nothing, and that's it. We can moan all we want and make a big deal out of it, we can look at all the empty pans and panic, but where would that leave us? Nowhere.' Well, what else can we do?' he asked. So I told him: 'We can pretend that all of this is normal, be satisfied with what we have, and enjoy every slice of bread as if it were a juicy steak.' That was it. We decided to stand tall and enjoy what we had. And, believe me, I really do enjoy everything. That's why I haven't lost weight. Why should I, when I have everything? If need be, I have meat, and cheese, and wine. . . . The arrangement between 'the two of us' is that we keep going like this until next May."

"But 'next May' already went by."

"That's true, but then we had another meeting, I mean me and Babo, and decided to continue the regime. At least until next May."

"Till when? Which 'next May'?"

"Well, either until the day we see some of that prewar meat on our table or one of us gives up. Or, God forbid, until something else happens, either to him or to me."

To Die in Sarajevo

I clearly remember how uneasy we felt coming out of the Dubrovnik cinema after the premiere of Bato Čengić's film *Silent Gunpowder* two years before the war. Nobody before him had fathomed the evil smouldering within those people, gathered on the hills like flocks of animals, turning their basest passions into ideological rituals. Before Bato, no one had ever revealed the meaning of the badges peasants used to wear on their hats, or hinted at the possible consequences of the rampant mythomania that gripped them. *Silent Gunpowder* was shot in a village only about thirty miles from Sarajevo, but to us the story could have taken place thirty light years away. We were truly naive, like kids who couldn't grasp what his camera showed us. We've gotten where we are today because of our infantile stupidity and innocence, without our kids, with no future. We didn't really deserve anything better.

Bato Čengić, someone who went through life, both personally and as a filmmaker, breaking through walls with his head, stayed in Sarajevo during the war. He stayed, somehow lost between what he knew before any of us and what has happened to us since. In *Silent Gunpowder* he showed us what was coming, just as he had done thirty years earlier in *Little Soldiers* and *My Family's Role in the Socialist Revolution.* He's gotten old, and his hair is completely white now. He lives in a house at the edge of the city, right between the hill where the maternity hospital used to be and the hill where the cemetery used to be. In a panic he calibrates the juice left in his car battery, jealously guarding it for the first, second, seventh, eighth, and fiftieth news program about what is happening to us and what will happen. Yet he knows, he knows very well, both about what happened and what will happen.

He has become more and more guilt-ridden over what he could have but didn't do for his little daughter Lana and his son Mak, the "Parrot" as he lovingly used to call him. So he submerged himself, maybe even unconsciously, into their world, and wholly identified himself with the thoughts and senses, the feelings and hopes, the fears and joys of those two children whose eyes remained—thanks to the "big people"—nailed to the valley between the maternity hospital and the graveyard, overgrown with weeds. Told in their thoughts, this is Bato's story . . . and if it were for real, its title would be "To Die in Sarajevo."

"I have been called Parrot since I was very little. Every time visitors came to our house and patted me and my cross-eyed sister on the head and pinched our cheeks, they asked us how we were. I answered 'Fine' and, as they slumped down into comfortable leather armchairs, I told them that the big, swan-shaped house on the nearby hill was where me and my little sister were born. I know that the grown-ups call it the Maternity Hospital. While our mothers giggled and pronounced the name of the hospital with a special emphasis, my sister and I would exchange secret glances and wait. We knew they would start talking about the storks that bring babies into this world. . . . My silly sister always roared with laughter because we had known for a long time how we were born. And that's the end of my parrot story about the Maternity Hospital, and the big window through which we can see the white building like a still life in a frame. At least that's how my dad talks about it.

"On the opposite side of our living room we have another big window, which opens onto the balcony and through which we can see the cemetery full of tall cypresses and slender birch trees. It often happened that, just as we were having dinner, sad music from brass instruments drifted through the air. It was played by members of the unshaven cemetery orchestra, marching unevenly. You know, the orchestra is usually followed by people in black crying over their loved ones. Then we could hear them say how the deceased had been kind and nice and the rest of the stuff that grown-ups lie about. It was then that father, usually so quiet, would get up angrily and shut the double window; then there was dead silence. Sometimes we could hear, through the closed windows, the blast of a military salute. Then my sister and I knew it was a national hero who had died! And when visitors would come to our place, pat us on the head and ask what's new, I told them, in my parrot way, that they were shooting again yesterday because a national hero had died. Then they began to talk about things we didn't understand—about war.

"I mean, that's how we grew up, my beautful cross-eyed sister and I, not really understanding what the grown-ups were talking about.

"But even now, there are many things I don't understand. Why did those on the hills blow the place we were born apart with rockets? Now it's an empty house with no glass in the windows and the roof burnt off, with no doctors, no grown-ups with flowers in their hands, without us, screaming children . . . Now it's ugly, completely destroyed, a maternity hospital for ducklings. The other side isn't even a cemetery anymore either. Nobody has buried anyone there for a long time, kids or grown-ups. Because the snipers on the hills shoot at funeral processions. I saw grown-ups hiding behind marble tomb-stones from our balcony, I saw them hide in panic under the flying stone angels and human figures to save their heads from the bullets. That's why the cemetery died. No more music. Now it's a big park full of tall grass and wild flowers where monuments to the dead have long since become invisible. Now the angels hover over the tall grass and cry. No grown-up goes into that dead cemetery any more, because the soldiers on the hills start shooting at once. And let me also say, all the cypresses and birch trees are gone because they were cut down at night by grown-ups one winter, after they had already burnt up every other piece of wood and all their furniture.

"There, that's how my little sister and I are growing up in this war.

"Yesterday was my birthday. There was no birthday cake or candles. My mother, who cries more and more often, says: 'Poor kids, they haven't had anything to eat for a long time. They look like walking skeletons from an anatomy book.' My mom knows what skeletons look like, since she's a doctor. Kids my age piss in their pants laughing at the word *skeletons!*

"At the end of the birthday party we really had a great time. We saw a feature-length movie for children. I think it was called *To Die in Madrid!*"

Bato's children are no longer with him. They left Sarajevo with their mother several months after the beginning of the war. They thought they'd stay together till the end, at whatever cost. Then, one night, Parrot wet his bed. From fright. They left while Bato stayed behind, constantly trying to guess what Lana and Parrot were thinking. He started thinking like them. Like a child. In spite of that horrifying, boring, cynical, false and idiotic news on the radio early in the morning, late in the morning, later in the morning, at noon, in the afternoon . . . news that is not childlike at all.

Enjoy Jail

Bojan and Dada Hadžihalilović are the remaining duo of the design group Trio that brought Sarajevo closer to the latest centers of "wild" graphic design, before and especially during the war. The third member of the trio, Lejla, managed to get out of Sarajevo and join her husband in Switzerland. Their friends who stayed behind hoped they would have a baby soon, so they could reform the "trio." Bojan and Dada, who got married during the war, continued working, constantly preoccupied with the question that haunts the dreams and the reality of everyone in Sarajevo: to leave or to stay.

"In late February 1993 we decided for the first and, so far at least, the last time, to go on a "business trip," the way others here already had. We planned to do it by night, running, crawling, rolling across the airport runway that was supposedly under UN protection but was actually controlled by the Serbian army. We made long preparations for the trip and, on the day set for it, arrived, half dead from fear, near the first wire barrier of the airport around six o'clock in the evening. About a mile across the runway was the beginning of the hilly road to freedom, either to the south or into northern Bosnia, whichever way you felt like going. On our side of the barrier they pushed some blue cards into our hands, cut in zigzag shapes with some numbers on them; they pointed to the wire in front of us and said: Now scram, it's over there, . . .'

"By this time we had no idea where we were, where we were going, or where we would end up; the only thing we were aware of was a roaring noise coming from the weapons all around us. That night we tried to get across the runway about five times, but UN-PROFOR stopped us every time. Finally, around three in the morning, we gave up on the whole idea and, completely frozen, miserable, dead tired and scared out of our wits, we went back home. For a whole year after that, we never stopped laughing at ourselves for what we did that night. Thousands of women and children, old people, cows and sheep managed to cross the runway, only Dada and Bojan didn't. But it doesn't matter. We must have really wanted to fail deep down, and it forced us to think of more ingenius ways to reach the outside world, since we couldn't do it physically. That old tune of Sarajevens who had left saying it was more important to get out and do something for Sarajevo from the outside than to stay kept nagging us. Then we started doing things with some posters; we would fax them around town when there was electricity. I guess the great idea was born from this, our idea of making postcards that would fool the UNPROFOR people, the journalists, the chetniks, and everyone else. . . . It's art, it's tiny, and we can get it out to do the 'work' for us. . . .

"And that's what happened. The postcards got off the ground and were quite a splash, but we couldn't free ourselves of the bug to get out of here. Then, finally, we hit on the real trick that would solve all our problems. One of the first postcards we did had 'Enjoy Sarajevo' on it, imitating the classical logo 'Enjoy Coca-Cola.' Everything was the same, the color, the lettering, the renowned curved line, the whole thing. So we thought Coca-Cola might sue us for plagiarism which, for them, of course, is serious business. Everyone we told this story to simply broke up: Why should you give a damn, what can they do to you, let them come to Sarajevo and arrest you! Of course, if they came to arrest us, then we'd really be in business. You can just imagine: Coca-Cola wins a suit against us for one or two million dollars, and we're totally broke. Then the court says: If you don't have the money, you'll get life, or let's say twenty years. We send our address to the American cops with detailed instructions about how to get from the airport to our house, because the roundabout way is treacherous and we don't want the poor cops to get shot by a sniper. They come to get us—in Reeboks, with handcuffs, the works. Our friends would eat their hearts out. And since America, or so they say, is a democratic country, we'd get put in some minimum security jail in California where we'd have everything we need to keep working. All we need is electricity, two computers and a printer. All the rest we have. They don't need to worry about the symptoms of any negative emotional reactions about being in jail, homesickness, and that kind of stuff. As it is we've been in jail for two years and we go from bed to bed as we move around Sarajevo looking for a place with electricity. We've been here for six months now, we sleep on desks and in sleeping bags, and we're quite sure that, as far as these things go, we'd be better off in any 'democratic jail.' You can't imagine all the things we could do if we just had some peace and quiet and a little electricity. You eat three times a day, you go for a walk in the courtyard, and—no snipers. That suit by Coca-Cola would be like Disneyland for us. Unfortunately, there's one little problem. We've heard that there are separate jails for men and women in America. And we refuse to be separated. If we wanted that, we could have gotten out of here a long time ago. So we have to come up with something that will keep us together. And we will, I know we can. . . ."

A Picture for Our Friends

Last summer, during a lull in the bombing, we crawled out like lizards in front of the café, and just sat in the sun. Nobody had a penny in his or her pocket, we could barely scrape up enough for one of those disgusting drinks. Then we started joking, laughing, just like in the old days. And, lo and behold, here comes Mišo, from the TV station. Mišo the Great. With his dyed hair and his camera, he just gets on his bike and shoots. He came over and pointed his camera at us. The guys started needling him: Mišo, how's your hair doing? Mišo, where're your chicks from tennis; when does the new course begin? But he just went on filming. Then one of us asked:

"Mišo, who are you doing this for?"

"For some pals in Sweden, so they can see us, so they can see how we're doing."

"What is there to see? Here we are, almost as if we were alive. . . . What do you say?"

Mario Kopić, economist, 33

Between Two River Banks

The news was absolutely incredible, absolutely unreal, and yet horribly cruel: they cut off the eternal stone rainbow over the Neretva, they destroyed the Old Bridge of Mostar that, for hundreds of years, had been so much more than a simple crossing from one bank to the other. It was then that I remembered Afan Ramić, a painter from Sarajevo and the greatest admirer of Mostar among all the painters who lived and worked outside that city. After losing his only son, Afan also lost the Old Bridge in the war. Can you imagine a greater loss?

It often seemed to me that rocky Herzegovina existed only for Afan and his paintings, whose every scent and every color seem to flow to the south. I even used to imagine that the superb emerald Neretva mysteriously flowed only for the sake of this bridge and for the sake of Afan's paintings. After that horrible news—which is still totally unbelievable not only to the people of Mostar but to everyone outside of Mostar as well—it seemed that Afan simply couldn't survive this second blow. But that wouldn't take into account his perseverance, always one step ahead of the tragedies that strike him. And when his son became part of the brigade of twenty-year-olds who perished as a blood sacrifice under the tanks just outside Sarajevo, Afan responded to this dreadful destiny with his paintbrush. He prepared an exhibition the likes of which had not been seen in Sarajevo since the beginning of the war. When the rainbow of Mostar ended up in the flowing rapids of the river below it, Afan turned to his canvasses, intimating the immortality of the link between the two river banks which could never remain separated. This time he did something more than what palette and paintbrush usually allow. He spoke to the people of Mostar, gathered in Sarajevo to bid a final farewell to their Bridge:

"One day when we set out to visit Mostar, what are we to say to the city, to this city without its bridge, what are we to say to our friends who have been so cruelly bereaved of their beauty, what are we to say to this river bereft of the roof over its head? There will be total silence at the point where the Old Bridge once stood, that elegant stone rainbow which, for centuries, was the very symbol of Eastern architecture in these lands, but also a synonym of the city on the emerald Neretva. Now the river flows under nothing, flows toward its delta through a dark black hole and goes away into nothingness. . . .

"A Nobel-prizewinner from the West once said, very poetically: 'Thought was born in the East of consciousness.' I have always felt that this architectural jewel was a kind of arrested metaphor, whose path was destined to begin in the East and consummate its beauty precisely in this place, on the cliffs of this very canyon, over this very river, and only here, in this land. It is hard, practically impossible, to imagine another place, another river, or another meaning of such a poetic image, for what would it mean elsewhere, what message could it possibly convey, why would it exist at all, if not here, in its own place?

"Besides its architectural beauty, the Mostar bridge linked not only two river banks but two civilizations that intertwine at precisely this point where the cultures of East and West have been destined to permeate each other for centuries. That mutual permeation of cultures embodies the dignity of the peoples who know Bosnia and Herzegovina as their only shared country. Only then can we understand the shock and amazement before this crime of biblical proportions, in this heroic landscape, before the destruction of this edifice, of this bridge, which is in and of itself the link between everything that exists between these two cultures. What are we to think when we realize that this act has come from people who have lived together like brothers for centuries, who are part of the same civilization, the same culture, the same family?

"An Arab writer from the thirteenth century once wrote down a beautiful thought about another part of the world: 'All things in the world are afraid of time, while in Egypt time is afraid of the Pyramids. . . .' Because of the ephemeral nature and brevity of human life, the pyramids were constructed for eternity. And I have always felt that the beauty of the stone metaphor of the Old Bridge, just because of its artistic perfection, will also live for eternity. And it will! It is easy to shoot at the poet, the builder. It is easy to take aim at a metaphor. But creative thought, whether it comes from the East or the West, the North or the South, cannot be annihilated. That shot at the Old Bridge was a shot at the heart of Herzegovina, at the heart of Mostar, at our Eastern heritage, at the Mostar of our childhood. Alas, for it was also a shot at the culture of those who have decided to kill the metaphor. But thought will live on, because it is inscribed in eternity."

Afan Ramić, this man from Sarajevo, from Mostar, from Počitelj, from the Adriatic island of Mljet, a man from all of our places, past and present, responded to the attack on metaphor with a new, magnificent exhibition. Magnificent because of the feelings woven into the paintings, magnificent because of the feelings of those who saw the paintings. His passage to the other bank of the Neretva could not be stopped by the plunging of the stone vertebrae into the river. Afan will always be able to get to the other side by walking on the reflection of the bridge, left in the Neretva to remain there forever. No shell or dynamite can touch it. The only problem is that the men with the dynamite know nothing of such things.

My Sister and the Others

"He's an honest man, that Marko Vešović, good for him! His face is as clean as gold. I'd give him my last crust of bread," said an old woman, hunched over as she stood in line for her daily ration of ten ounces of bread. She had just read his article, published in *Oslobodenje* two days after the massacre at Markale, about his former colleagues, professors at the Philosophy Faculty of Sarajevo. They had been living "up there" in Pale for two years where—as he put it—they "specialized in remote-control slaughter by shelling."

Everybody else in Sarajevo spoke of Marko the same way. A writer and professor, he was a Montenegran who had become one with the Miljacka and the people of this city. He didn't become so popular by doing things unexpectedly or on impulse. He always spoke in an even, steady way—whether it was when he was nominated to be a member of the Presidency of Bosnia and Herzegovina and he brushed the politicians off with great dignity, when he dealt with ordinary people, or when he got into arguments with corrupt wheelers and dealers at the top. A quiet, dignified neighborhood man with disheveled curly black hair, by nature kind to a fault, his language the envy of every writer, Marko Vešović. A month and a half after the first shells hit Sarajevo, on May 30, 1992, he wrote in *Oslobodenje*.

"Yesterday, at least for me, was the saddest of all the fifty or so days from the beginning of the siege of Sarajevo. Because I got a call from my sister in Montenegro. She called to attack me for apparently being on the opposite side of the murderer from Durmitor [a high mountain in Montenegro, the birthplace of Radovan Karadžic]. Instead of asking me 'Brother, do you have anything to eat?,' she went to great lengths to explain, as if she were speaking to a blind man, what was *really* happening in Sarajevo. Instead of asking me 'How late did you stay in the shelter last night?' or 'Does your ulcer hurt from general Mladić's rockets?', she just exclaimed: 'The whole world is against the Serbs. Well, we'll screw the world!'

"I listened, dumbfounded. I was about to say, 'Hey, woman, I am your brother. . . . What are Karadžić and Milošević to us?' But I just couldn't utter a word. My mouth turned to lead.

"There you go, I said to myself, hanging up. That's what those flies from under Milošević's tail have done to people with their propaganda on television, on the radio, and in the newspapers. Two years, daily, methodically, they've been brainwashing people. And what's the upshot? A sister who, though hardly literate, is frantically eager to teach her brother, a writer, what he will say and what he will write. No wonder, then, that fresh hordes of volunteers are swarming daily from Serbia and Montenegro into Bosnia. Who wouldn't go to fight when—according to Milošević—they are killing Serbs here like flies. Here, the Serbian people is fighting for its survival. True, in the struggle to save their skin, the Serbs have obliterated one Bosnian town after another. Defending their age-old hearths, they have conquered seventy percent of this country's territory. In order to save ourselves from this imaginary danger, we have made a dozen concentration camps for Muslims all over Bosnia and Herzegovina.

"Nothing short of a magic wand will erase the poison that Milošević poured into the heads of the Orthodox people in the Balkans. And the dose is big enough to take us all down by collective suicide.

"For the fact that the entire world is against Milošević is not in the least an indictment against the butcher from Dedinje [a residential quarter of Belgrade mostly inhabited by VIPs]. On the contrary, if everybody hates him, that's reason enough for all of us to perish under his banner. Oh Lord, have mercy on us!

"On one side, then, are the good and honest Serbs, on the other—the remaining vicious world. And we'll really fuck up that world if it doesn't leave us alone—so we can bomb maternity hospitals in peace. The phone rings again. A friend from Belgrade wants to know what the destroyer of Sarajevo, general Mladić, has done this time. Then he says, 'Can't you somehow escape to Belgrade?' And I reply, 'As long as the capital is ruled by a fascist from a village in Montenegro, I can come to Belgrade only one way—in a tank.' "

Marko Vešović is still in Sarajevo, two years after this letter. The possibility of going to Belgrade, by hook or by crook, never materialized. The world is taking good care of its favorite baby, Slobodan Milošević, and his cronies from Durmitor and Pale. Nobody even tries to phone Marko any more. At any rate, it hasn't even been possible for a long, long time now. Those who have to say something to him do so face-to-face, in the streets of Sarajevo. Man to man, as is fitting among human beings. That seems to be the best and the most beautiful way. For Marko, and certainly for Sarajevans too.

A Great Ordinary Man

Before the war, Brigadier General of the Army of Bosnia and Herzegovina, Jovan Divjak, known to friends and acquaintances as Jovo, was a colonel of the former Yugoslav People's Army. A Serb from Belgrade by birth, and second in command of the Bosnian Army, he is considered by many the most popular soldier in the city. Of course, like everything else, this can and has been argued after all that has happened to Sarajevo and the new saying: "The only good Serb is a dead Serb." But for Jovo, this poses no problem. After all, he himself has been saying "I wanted to be a Bosnian, but they wouldn't let me." Everyone in Sarajevo knows that Karadžić and Mladić hate to see Divjak in the delegation of the Bosnian Army because, by his very presence, he completely disarms their claim that coexistence between the three Bosnian ethnic groups was never possible in the past and will never be so in the future.

Jovo Divjak has always behaved in ways that subvert the most widely held preconceptions: that a soldier must be strict and not particularly interested in art and culture, that a soldier considers his rank and position very important, that a soldier loves hierarchy and firm discipline ... Serbian General Gvero, a former "colleague" from the days they spent together in the Yugoslav Army, asked Divjak to convert to Islam. Jovo responded, "No problem. I'll do it the day General Gvero climbs down the tree and straightens himself up." Soon after that, a British officer from the "blue helmets," dead serious the way they usually are, said to General Divjak: "General, Sir, I wish to inform you that, according to reliable sources, General

Gvero has been seen eating bananas these days." To Jovo Divjak, however, the joke was in bad taste. But he responded, half aloud, "What was said between Gvero and me is our affair. I thank the Brit for wanting to show that he is on our side, but I'd still prefer that he not get mixed up in it."

Jovo Divjak is best known by the soldiers on the front defense lines of Sarajevo, where he goes almost every night. After the soldiers, his closest comrades are the actors of Sarajevo's theaters, the painters, poets, and musicians. And, obviously, the journalists. This general without escort, without chauffeur or bodyguards, this general who shows journalists worried about fitness that he can stand on his head longer than they, is a man who keeps children's drawings and letters from strangers and soldiers in his office and has a precise answer to the question "Why have you remained in the Bosnian Army with your sons Želimir and Vladimir?" His answer is, in fact, this question: "Could there be anything more natural for a man who spent the best years of his life in Mostar, on the Neretva, in Sarajevo, and all over Bosnia? And why did *you* stay?"

Sarajevo remembers from the now legendary clips from May 3, 1992, when the "real" war started in Bosnia and Herzegovina. On that day the president of Bosnia-Herzegovina, Alija Izetbegović, after being "detained" in the Yugoslav Army barracks near the airport, was to be exchanged for General Kukanjac and his collaborators. The commander of the federal army was leaving Sarajevo at that very moment to launch a full-scale war. Divjak was the first to climb the armored vehicle with Izetbegović and Kukanjac inside it, and he asked the president: "Mister President, are you well, is everything all right, have they mistreated you?" This took place on Sarajevo's Street of Volunteers and it was Divjak who directed the whole operation, an operation that is sure to go down in the history of Bosnia and Herzegovina. On that day, in the uniform he had worn for decades, Divjak put himself on the side of those who were totally without defense. He knew why. He wasn't too concerned about what those around him thought. The soldiers with whom he shared his last cigarette, to whom he gave his binoculars and his gloves, when such things were hard to find, knew what he was up to. When they began to play games with the general, at a time when those kinds of games could be lethal, when they arrested him in Herzegovina for the sake of "his own security," I know soldiers who said: "We don't know what they are trying to pin on him but we know who he is and what he's about, and we'll get him out of it."

Back in Sarajevo, he told people who hugged and kissed him in the street: "Why are you so excited? If you were afraid what would happen to me and are happy to see me back, that means you suspected me." The pages of the diary which he kept during his "detention for security reasons," include the following entry: "The president came to the place where I was, near Buturović Polje. I don't know whether I hoped that he would come to see me or not. I think I rather didn't. Did he remember the Street of Volunteers and how I'd climbed up onto the armored car and said, "How are you, Mr. President? I'm fine thanks. I just don't know how my wife Vera is doing, and my sons Želimir and Vladimir, and my dear friends who are as important to me as my own life. How are they?"

To those dear friends, and to many others, the then Colonel and now General Divjak wrote a letter in *Oslobodenje* on December 20, 1992. Among other things, he wrote the following:

"My dear friends from Sarajevo . . . Since April 6, 1992, some people have been bothered by, and have not been able to understand, the fact that I, Jovan Divjak, have joined the ranks of the fighters for the freedom, territorial integrity and indivisibility of the Republic of Bosnia and Herzegovina. In the course of these nine months I have been mistrusted and suspected, my life has been threatened. Dear Sarajevan friends, you know me well: I was not, I am not, nor will I ever be a *chetnik*. Nobody can contest my right to fight with you, Muslims and Croats, with the citizens of Sarajevo and all of Bosnia and Herzegovina, for its freedom. I am not afraid of threats, but I *am* hurt by the heinous accusations and insults. I will not sell my honor to anybody. I will continue to fight and nobody can deprive me of the right to live in freedom and happiness, to remain on Logavina Street and walk along the Wilson Promenade . . ."

At the very beginning of the war, as I accompanied him on what was then a dangerous night inspection of Sarajevo's defense lines and the deserted corridors of the semidestroyed Maternity Hospital on the outskirts of the city, Jovo said to me: "You know, Zlatko, it wasn't some mock patriotism that made me stay here. It was just the most normal thing to do, I couldn't even imagine any other solution. Ever since I was a young man I wanted to do something more, something better, something more meaningful than is possible in ordinary life. . . ."

General Divjak, a Sarajevan pal, a jokester, and a bit of a bohemian, has done for Sarajevo and its people a great deal more than can be done in "ordinary life." The most important thing, however, is that he also remained an ordinary person, in the noblest sense of that word.

The Mayor and Magic Johnson

You could say that Muhamed Kreševljaković, the mayor of Sarajevo, is like a character from a joke. Not just any old joke, but from those typically Bosnian jokes about Suljo and Mujo [nicknames for Suleyman and Mustafa] in which every stupidity is readily forgiven and, most of all, understandable. Those in the know about all of the jokes that have been circulating in Sarajevo since the beginning of the war claim, quite "seriously," that the mayor indeed "participated" in a joke that has by now acquired legendary status.

Right at the beginning of the war, two Sarajevans heard that the *chetniks* were advancing toward Sarajevo from the direction of Pale. They decided to mount an ambush somewhere on the road, to welcome the enemy. The story has it that, after the news broke, the *chetniks* were supposed to show up at any minute, because they were already quite close. So the Sarajevans waited behind a tree. An hour passed, two hours—nothing. At the end of the third hour one of the two heroes—some bozos even say it was the mayor—turned to his "comrade in arms" and, with a worried look on his face, said: "You know what, buddy, those guys must have had something bad happen to them. Why don't you wait here while I go and see, maybe the poor guys need some help. . . ."

The story about the mayor and his "encounter" with Magic Johnson during the Olympic Games in Barcelona is not too different from the one above, but its authenticity is guaranteed. The Sarajevan delegation, which included Mayor Kreševljaković, met at a reception during the Games with members of the American Olympic basket-ball team. Delighted to be in the vicinity of the great Johnson, Kreševljaković persuaded the delegation's interpreter, a serious lady, to go up to the famous player and ask him to pose for a photo with the Bosnian flag in his hand. "Our people in Sarajevo will be thrilled when they see it. Come on, you have to persuade him to do it," the mayor insisted. The woman finally went over to Johnson and told him about the mayor's request. He explained politely that the waving of flags or any such things was under the strict supervision of the sponsor who financed him, and that it would cost him dearly. It was not that he didn't want to do it, on the contrary, but it was a question of contracts, principles, etc. Having heard a precise transla-tion of all this, the mayor still wouldn't abandon his plan: "Go ahead, tell him everybody in Sarajevo will go crazy with excitement, to hell with the sponsors, they'll understand, I know for sure, they're nice people. Explain that to him, I know he's a great man, he'll understand."

The interpreter went to see Magic Johnson once again. He was still hesitating a little bit and then, generously, said: "OK, let's do two quick shots, just make it fast. Where's the flag?"

She rushed back to the mayor to tell him that the great Johnson had agreed, and asked for the flag.

"The flag, what flag? You think I have a flag on me? Do you think I carry flags around in my pockets? You better tell the guy we can do it tomorrow, nice and slow, like real gentlemen. At ease, without all the rush. I knew he was a great guy. . . ."

In Sarajevo, much later, this story about Hamo the Mayor [nickname for Muhamed] was told with great delight. It was generally agreed that he did everything in his power to promote the Bosnian flag. That there wasn't one around wasn't his fault.

Pilot in the Slammer

Aša flew small planes. Just like that, for the hell of it, for his own pleasure. He learned to fly because he was the doctor at the airport so his friends from the aviation school talked him into flying with them. A long time ago he used to be a race-car driver. He once got as far as Monte Carlo. As a doctor he worked all over, from Sarajevo to Iraq. "God, what bad luck I had over there in Iraq. The nurses were all ugly as hell. . . ."

When his father was a big shot in the government, in those far-away, happier times, Aša was a taxi driver in Sarajevo. Everyone around him said that it was only a game, that he was posing, but Aša just kept at it. Then he was a doctor again, a gynecologist, then a specialist in pharmacology, and lots of other things. Just before the war, he, his wife Enisa, their daughters Inka and Dina and their cocker spaniel Briči, opened up a video rental store called Indi. In the neighborhood we all thought the name had something to do with Kon Tiki, with faraway seas and closer nostalgias, but it was actually just a combination of the first syllables of his daughters' names. At Indi you could get tapes of great movies, drink great coffee, play a good game of billiards, and hear great jokes.

When the war broke out—just as Aša finished a project that turned the space around the house, to the astonishment of his neighbors, into a big open-air restaurant—the Indi became a gathering place of genuine UNPROFOR men and their entourage of women. It was the place where the most serious tales of the surrounding battles were told and where Enisa made the greatest pizzas that could possibly be made out of nothing, garnished with a lot of love and the memories of Aša's flying and racing days. An old mini-Fiat was used to make a natural–gas power generator, but there was never any gas. An ordinary boiler part was converted into a device for regulating the pressure in an espresso machine, infusion needles and tubes combined with God knows what else produced lamps . . . and life continued. The mongrels in the neighborhood started going after their cocker spaniel, the incredible Brič, but neither she nor Aša let them hang around. The former pilot, this eternal amateur of altitude, became, slowly but surely, the city's top specialist in sniffing gas mains to find out whether any gas was seeping through from somewhere.

Enisa was growing thinner by the day, the patrons of the café Indi had emptier and emptier pockets, the older daughter, Inka, was becoming more beautiful and spending more time in the "neighborhood" while the younger Dina was getting more nostalgic over memories of her friends from school; she spent more and more time with Brič, "this superb young lady that helped my kids stay sane," as Aša used to say.

It seemed as if, slowly but surely, everything was going downhill. The UNPROFOR men with their overdressed "high-class" female escorts were seen less and less, no more pizzas could be made, and the smell of gas could be detected less and less frequently. There were fewer and fewer boards to make fire with from the "Austrian House," that place they had built for their team during the Winter Olympics and then donated to Sarajevo . . . and, finally, shells found their way to Aša's Indi. One fell across the street, another a little farther up, yet another down the street, and so on until fear gripped even Aša the pilot.

Then, one day, it all came to a breaking point. Or at least it should have, considering that fear is a basic human feeling and that, in times like this, gratuitous arrests and overnight detentions cannot be taken as a sign of enlightened revolutionary activity. Aša and his last guests, gathered around a single bottle of French wine—acquired God knows

how and saved for a long time—were taken from his own café, the
Indi, to a rather distant police station to spend the night "because they
were found in a restaurant (i.e., a public facility) after the curfew (i.e.,
10 P.M.)." What had seemed totally incomprehensible to a man who,
all his life, viewed things from the sky above or raced ahead along the
world's tracks and trails, was simply taken for granted by the kids in
uniform: article of law number so and so, paragraph number so and
so, and that's it! Then the slammer, the cops, the isolation, sleeping on
a table, just because you were in your own house, with friends, with a
bottle of wine.

A popular old song of Sarajevo's legendary group Indexi goes:
"Even a fall is a flight . . ." For Aša the pilot, the night in jail was not
actually a fall because he himself had decided, from his soaring
heights, not to let it be a fall but a flight. That night, in that same jail,
we heard the story that had always been effective with women in the
old days: "There was a mother who had two daughters, one was the
most beautiful girl in the world. She never gave herself to anyone and
had a lot of bad luck. The other was playful and free in every sense of
the word, but always lived happily with the best of luck . . ." He also
told us this police station would be a lot better off if, for example, they
had a little coffee and a few drinks to sell to those errant souls in
Sarajevo who were caught after 10 P.M. "in a public place or peram-
bulating the city's public spaces . . ." We saw pictures of Aša in the
cockpit and heard everything about the ugly nurses in Iraq. "If you've
never been in prison, then you're not a revolutionary," he said to
comfort us and asked the commander of the police station to make
just one phone call to Enisa, Inki, Dina and Briči, so they wouldn't
worry. "That little bitch didn't even bark when we left. From tomorrow it's only rice for her, without meat. Even a penguin would have
barked if it had seen how the police were taking me out of my house."

Then at five in the morning, when they let him and his guests out
after the curfew, he went back to the Indi, smelled the gas which
wasn't there, and made coffee with bits and pieces of the "Austrian

House." There wasn't even a trace of dawn, just darkness, winter, and snow. . . .

A few hours later that same day, he met me on the street and said: "Zlaja, if you haven't eaten anything, if you're hungry, go to Enisa, she made a beautiful pie. I'm going to work at the Ministry of Health, after that, maybe, I'll go to the airport where there's supposed to be some talks with those from the other side about sharing some water taps. Tonight, at the usual time, I'll see you at the Indi. We'll close up at ten, so the youngsters don't have any problems with us. Maybe Enisa can make a pizza, if there's any raw material. Come on, Zlaja, don't stand us up, you know that revolutionaries always have to meet in secret after they get out of the slammer—we have to study the materials we have. You know how many countries there are about which we have said absolutely nothing. And how many more ugly nurses. Hey, man, maybe we'll cook up a plan to open a bistro in the slammer. I have a feeling we're gonna go back there soon. It sure seems like it. . . ."

At that point Slavenko Šehović, known as Aša, Health Inspector of the Republic of Bosnia and Herzegovina, pilot, race-car driver, owner of the Indi, and a professional natural-gas sniffer, went down the street to work. From there, perhaps he went to the airport, where he belongs, where people keep taking off so they can look at life from up above with a bird's eye view, as is only fitting for such men.

". . . and just wait and see what will happen when all this is over with, and when the mice run away."

That night, we discussed one more sunny country with beautiful shores. We stayed long after ten o'clock. They didn't come to get us, though the door wasn't locked. Briči managed, once again, to save the honor of the house, to the satisfaction of Aša, Enisa, Inka and Dina, and their Sarajevan buddies. Gas and electricity were nowhere to be "found," but it didn't matter. To fall is also to fly.

The Vase

"... On May 28, 1992, you know, the night they were destroying Sarajevo, my apartment was practically demolished. A grenade passed through the kitchen into the living room and exploded there, turning everything to rubble. Me, my wife and my daughter were in the basement, and I remember how sorry I was to have to go when the shelling started because they were showing that great series "The Winds of War" on TV. Things had just gotten to the boiling point in the Pacific, and I couldn't wait to see what would happen next. After an awful explosion that rocked the whole house, I realized it couldn't have been too far from our apartment, but we didn't dare go upstairs the whole night. The next day, when everything quieted down a little, I realized in despair that everything was gone. Hundreds of little things that we cherished, each little thing connected to some memory—photographs, various objects we had brought home from our trips. Simply not knowing what to do with myself, I walked out into the street, now full of debris, partly burned rafters and pieces of furniture from other houses. People were picking up what they could, trying not to get entangled in the cables dangling off the nearby electric poles. A huge stream, coming out of a water pipe hit by a shell, ran down the street.

"By some miracle, except for the broken windows, the Leonardo gallery on the other side of the street remained relatively intact. The owner, my friend Pajo, was walking around in circles, unable to decide where to start cleaning and tidying up. I walked in and immediately spotted a beautiful little vase: a vase like that in the old days would hardly have been noticed in a nicely furnished apartment. But now, just like in more normal times, I thought I should buy the vase, simply because I liked it. I asked Pajo, in what to him must have been the most incredible voice in the world, how much the vase was. He stared at me for a couple of seconds, then waved me off dismissively and kept on working. I found it strange that he didn't answer. I asked him again, again he stared at me in disbelief, and then, turning back to his work, said, more to himself, 'What do I know how much it costs today. It used to cost five hundred dinars, as far as I can remember. . . .' I put the vase under my arm, as if making sure no one else would come along to grab such a bargain, and walked out of the store saying to Pajo, 'I'll be right back, I'm going home to get some money.'

"And that's how it was. My wife, still in the basement, had some money on her. I didn't tell her what I needed it for. Who knows how she would have reacted! When I brought the vase to the basement and told people where I got it, everyone had something to say. One neighbor told me I was crazy, but that she, being so wise, 'understood my situation' very well. There was pity in her eyes, especially when she looked at my daughter. Some people didn't say anything, but it was clear to them that I was even more of an idiot than the first neighbor had dared to say. My wife was also silent, but in a different way. Only my seventeen-year-old daughter took up the vase, looked at it curiously, and said, 'Thanks a lot for buying it, Dad. I've been looking at it at Pajo's for a long time. We have to find a safe place for it in the apartment.' "

"We spent days cleaning up the apartment, at least trying to make what was left somewhat livable. As we cleaned, we discussed where the safest place for the vase would be. It was more than obvious that there wasn't such a place—three walls of our apartment faced three different sides from which shells whistled every day. Still, we acted as if the wall with the gaping hole from a shell were the only unsafe place while everywhere else, of course, would have to be more secure.

Finally, we found the safest place in the apartment, and that vase is still there. I'm completely convinced now that we have never had anything more important in our house. And I'm truly happy I could buy something I liked."

Refik Beširević, film technician, 48

An Unheard-of Wonder

Sulejman Klokoči, a young man from Kosovo, came to Sarajevo just before the war, as a cameraman for Yutel, a TV station which was supposed to be "Yugoslav." He came with a great technical reputation, open eyes and an open heart. Sulejman's father had given another task to his friends in Sarajevo: to find a match for his son with a Bosnian woman so he could get married and settle down. Instead of spending a few months in what was then the most open, freest city in Yugoslavia, Sulejman ended up staying in the world's biggest concentration camp for two years. His friends couldn't find a Bosnian girl for him to marry—they simply didn't get around to it because of the war and the catastrophe that needed to be documented daily by camera. But Sulejman Klokoči, drawing his own conclusions and without any big speeches, became more than a Bosnian son-in-law. He became a genuine Sarajevan.

The night before going back home to Kosovo, to see his mother and father for the first time in two years, this giant of a man spoke from the heart, at the brink of tears:

"Now, before leaving and after everything that happened, I think I'm more of a Sarajevan than a lot of people who were born here. And I feel sad, sadder then I've ever felt in my whole life. After I finished at the university, I wandered around the world for twelve years, through all kinds of battlefields, only to find my home here. I don't know what it is in me that stopped me from leaving Sarajevo earlier to see my family, even though I wanted to see them so much. I don't know where or who I am. My family is there, but everything I have is here. There is no scale that can weigh all this. Sarajevo is a wonder. When I first came here, it was raining downtown, everything was dark and murky. I went to the television building, and it was sunny there. I couldn't figure it out. What kind of a city is this, with rain and sunshine at the same time in the same place, with the past and the future in the same place at the same time, with so many unbelievable differences, and still, everything is like one? Different but the same every moment. Cold, warm, old, and new, but everything so powerful . . . And even when I leave Sarajevo, I won't know if I will ever learn who or what Sarajevo is. What kind of people are these Sarajevans, why are they so special? Someone I know here, just in passing, asked me if I had enough money for my trip home, since I have to go through Italy and Albania. I told him I had enough for coffee and a few drinks, that it would be enough. But he put his hand in his pocket, took out five hundred marks, and pushed the money into my hand: 'Here,' he said, 'for the trip, just in case . . .' I don't even know the guy's name, but he's a Sarajevan. So tell me, where else can you find that, in the midst of war and misery? My heart aches so much for the people here, and yet at the same time I'm so proud of them."

Sulejman Klokoči, master cameraman, and a master of heart and soul, now a Sarajevan, left only to come back home. Before getting on the white armored vehicle to take him to the airport, he said, "I'm infected by this city and there's no cure. Now I can say I'm truly happy because I'm a Sarajevan." On his way back he'll have to pass through barricades set up by creatures who've never been able to stop any of Sulejman's friends, nor poison their souls. It was dark and foggy at the airport that day, but the sun was out in the center of town.

A Letter to Akira Kurosawa

In the name of Allah, the Beneficent, the Merciful!

Dear Mr. Akira Kurosawa,

I have wanted to write you a letter for a long time. I am sorry that I cannot use anything else but words to write it with. I wish I could use something more dignified than words, but I can't . . .

Actually, I don't like writing letters. Although I used to write, I don't like that now either. Now I like to read.

My whole life—and I'm fifty-three now—I have remembered your films.

I saw *Rashomon* for the first time when I was just a kid.

I don't remember my father because he was killed when I was three years old, but I do remember my uncle Omer. When I was about thirty, Uncle Omer died. I remember my uncle Omer the same way I remember *Rashomon,* and the other way around. . . . What I want to say is that I love my uncle and that's why I remember him. I've seen thousands of films in my life, and met thousands of people, but I don't remember either the films or the people.

But I remember your films, even though I haven't seen all of them.

What is a film? A film is something very suspicious.

What is art? Who knows!

But you are the only one, Akira Kurosawa, who has made film into art.

Your films are the jewels of my innermost life. And only because your films are the jewels of my innermost life do I have the courage to write you this letter.

If the whole world, millions and millions of people, say, "Akira Kurosawa!" my cry, "Akira Kurosawa!" will not be heard even as a whisper. But I would still want to say, "Akira Kurosawa!" because I am only what you wanted me to be while watching your films.

That's what I am.

Now, I would like to ask your permission to say something.

I see three countries and three armed nations surround my country and my unarmed nation disappearing before my very eyes. I see Europe looking on with indifference, and I see Europe disappearing too.

I see Japan, distant in all its beauty!

I wouldn't like Japan to disappear either.

So, if you happen to know Mr. Yasushi Akashi, please tell him to stop acting like Mr. Boutros Boutros Ghali, the UN pharaoh's exotic houseboy.

Sincerely yours,

NEDŽAD IBRIŠIMOVIĆ
President of the Writers' Association
of Bosnia-Herzegovina

Nedžad wrote this letter on Thursday, February 10, 1994. Whether or not it got to Japan is anyone's guess, but Yasushi Akashi still obeys Mr. Boutros Boutros Ghali.

Rice by Candlelight

Officially, Nermina Zildžo is a conservationist at the Art Gallery of Bosnia and Herzegovina. On the surface, she is a typical representative of that generation of Sarajevans in their forties who only have to say a few words to demonstrate their knowledge, charm, and singular sense of humor—everything that rightfully used to characterize "the Sarajevo spirit," now sought after by hundreds of journalists eager to verify the resilience of this city against all odds.

Unlike so many others in town, Nermina Zildžo could get out of Sarajevo during the war and take a whiff of the magic of peace and quiet. But she understands how impossible it is to tell the Sarajevo story to those who haven't been here. She could appreciate the meticulous attention people over there pay to the most banal things about our life here without, at the same time, making an effort to use simple logic to figure out simple truths and recognize obvious things. . . .

"We are not talking about politics. We are talking about ordinary, everyday life. When I first came out of Sarajevo in the summer of 1993, I was enthusiastically welcomed by a friend in Zagreb. We talked so much about Sarajevo—about the living conditions, the fear, the fighting, the food—that I got the impression she knew everything about us. Then she made dinner and loaded my plate with rice. I felt the room spinning around me. It wasn't until she saw me picking at the rice with my fork, halfway through dinner, that she realized what the problem was. And we've woven legends about how rice, spaghetti, and soy beans are already coming out of our ears! A few days later the same thing happened to me with spaghetti in Venice. My friends were just thrilled to immerse me in pasta, prepared a thousand different ways.

"Things came to a head in Paris, at a dinner given by a very respected and distinguished lady. She practically lives at the Louvre. I had never been in a place like hers. The guests, her friends, were not just plain folk. On the table . . . candles; on the plates . . . lentils, prepared in different ways, in huge amounts. Maybe in Paris it's elegant to eat rustic food from wooden plates with wooden utensils, but I was so nostalgic for civilization, for light. In Sarajevo, we used lentils to make coffee. . . .

"The next day I went to see a doctor: a friend arranged for me to get a shot against hepatitis. The doctor knew I had come from Sarajevo and that I would be going back. He gave me one shot immediately and another to take back to Sarajevo. As I was leaving he told me, without even thinking, that it was particularly important, over there in Sarajevo, not to forget to put the vaccine in the refrigerator. The refrigerator that runs on electricity! Another doctor, who even saw me ahead of his other patients because I was from Sarajevo, listened to me with great attention, and then advised me to avoid stressful situations when I get back home, to pay close attention to my diet, to eat lots of fruits and vegetables, to take vitamins . . .

"There it was, I realized that our story had been completely lost in time and space. Nothing can be explained to anybody, it's totally useless to talk. Later on I was sorry not to have asked that doctor if I could eat lots of ice cream and chocolate.

"My last evening in Paris was marvelous. Some friends gave me a farewell dinner . . . by candlelight! What a horror. But we shouldn't blame them. Their intentions were good, and life is ahead of them. They will learn . . ."

A City that Won't Die

For a long time one could not get to Skenderija, the sports and cultural center on "that" side of the Miljacka. Just above the arena that embodied so many glorious moments in its history, there was a sniper nest from which that part of the city had been terrorized for months. Even so, as far back as early 1993 there were rumors that every morning strange noises came from the Skenderija, that the clamor of competition resounded there, just like in the old days. Then the story spread that some diehards actually were playing soccer there, that tournaments had even been organized with teams from different parts of the city. Where and how these guys got into the arena was kept a secret for a long time. At the end of that year, the UNPROFOR men, especially the French, also started coming to the Skenderija, so the games reached an international level.

One day something happened that even the arena's own odd clientele considered a miracle. A real honest-to-God boxing tournament was organized, the stands were packed, and the sound of cheering crowds echoed all the way to the nearby hills, something "they" must have found totally baffling. Down there, crouching at ringside with a sly smile, was a man in a leather jacket with the crooked nose of a real boxer. His presence probably surprised everyone who knew this popular Sarajevan. Bakir Nakaš, director of the City Hospital, formerly the Military Hospital and later, briefly, the "French Hospital," was giving tips to two ten-year-olds skipping around the ring with gloves and helmets that seemed bigger than they were. Bakir had never been involved in sports before, "except in front of TV screens," as he himself said. Now he is the vice-president of a boxing club called the Golden Lily. This club, says Nakaš, brings together everyone hungry for life, all the citizens of a city that refuses to die.

In an arena that could only be reached by running across a bridge open to snipers but which still seethed with excitement the way it used to, in an almost surreal atmosphere, Dr. Nakaš told this simple story slowly, as if he were talking about the most common things in the most common times:

"They just want to prove that life here hasn't been demolished. Actually, they just need to prove this to themselves. Psychologically, the battle with 'those up there' is over. They can't do anything else to us. They are just an ugly reality, something we've gotten used to. The real question, which becomes more and more difficult, is to figure out whether you can survive and overcome all the suffering when you have nothing left but yourself. They've crammed us into cellars, into rat holes. But these kids want to live, even in cellars. They want to play, to compete and have hope, even down there, underground. That's how it is. Just like all those art exhibits in the hallways of apartment buildings, when there were no galleries and exhibition halls left. And the plays people perform in those same hallways. Everything is like that. The big shots who used to show up at glamorous places in black suits with invitations in their hands and badges on their lapels left a long time ago. Kids, ordinary people, heroes, and cripples have stayed. And they don't want to die. That's why sports, art, culture, music, laughter, anything that is human hasn't left the city but rooted itself even more firmly than before. Maybe what's going on now in the ring looks funny, I mean these kids and how seriously they take it. But they are like gods. They have absolutely nothing; not only don't they have the means to work, to train, they don't even have anything to eat. Many of them, literally, don't even have a roof over their heads, some of them don't even have parents anymore. And they hope to recover everything. They train like fanatics even though they know they'll never be great stars, great boxers. They simply come to play, hoping that something better will come along. Maybe some of them will even make it. People from outside who come to watch say this 'goes beyond reason.' That's because they don't know these kids or, for that matter, any of the rest of us. If they knew us, they wouldn't say that this is crazy or irrational. We simply refuse to die—as a city, as a people, as a future. I don't even care if this sounds pathetic or corny. That's just the way it is. They told me today that I'm crazy to walk around the ring with these kids. What else should I do? Sit around with who-knows-who and argue about politics: will they sign or not? Whether they do or don't, nothing will change for these kids. They have already won their battle. What else is there for me to do? Here, I'm looking at this ring to see if I can somehow take it to the hospital to organize a match for our patients. I can see how big it is and it's not going to be easy. We don't have a hall that size. But it doesn't matter. If I can't fit it somewhere inside, then I'll wait till summer and we'll set it up in the courtyard. We'll protect it somehow. In fact, that's how we showed *Hair* in the hospital. What is there 'beyond reason' in it? It seems so incredibly simple to me. If we only had a little more peace and electricity. A bit more water wouldn't hurt either. You have to wash up after the match, if you can. The kids love that."

We Are Alive . . .

Everybody in the world grew up with a song. Since time immemorial everybody has felt tremors at the sound of a voice and a tune which, like waves coming from the distance of childhood and youth, bring tender memories of more innocent days. During the past decades Sarajevo has grown up with the songs of Kemal Monteno, probably more than with anybody else's. His voice and his lyrics have been Sarajevo's air and water, our truth and our love; they were with us on our first dates, they explained everything when we had neither words nor explanations, they've said the most beautiful things we wanted but didn't know how or wouldn't dare pronounce. Even when we stole his lyrics, uttering them in the dark to those who turned us into little thieves, our thefts were pardoned, in the name of love.

And it goes without saying that Kemal Monteno remained in Sarajevo with his guitar and that perpetual smile on what has become a withered, skinny, and wrinkled face. Hungry, but without ever admitting it, alone, but without anyone knowing about it, and infinitely mad at a life that failed him and every song he wrote about Sarajevo. He stayed on to sing and bring out what is left of our tears which, miserable and humiliated though we are, we try to hide only to deprive the world of the pleasure of seeing us cry. During the nights, when we go through the toughest times, even though it's tough *all* the time, in the corners of former cafés and clubs his lyrics have been reaching out to us for months.

Our fingers are forgetting how to play,
our voices how to sing.
We no longer remember our lyrics,
dead guitars,
dead guitars . . .
Will those up there
be the only ones,
the only ones still singing?

On one of those nights, when we still believed that this crazy war was only a sad episode in our lives, he said to me, "They ask me why I don't write any songs. Well, I don't want to. I'll wait till I can write the most beautiful love song that can be written. Now, I can't write a love song. And I refuse to write any other kind."

For months after that, he and his inseparable friend Davorin Popović, the only other legend of Sarajevo and our youth that equals him, defied the hatred with their old lyrics. Nor did he ever allow the Singer—as he endearingly called Davorin—to sing anything unworthy of the times we were going through and the need of people to lean on their songs as if they were the only supporting pillars left in the wasteland of Sarajevo.

One day Kemal got a letter from Zagreb, an almost insurmountable distance by today's standards even though it used to be only a hop, skip and a jump away. The letter was from Arsen Dedić, an old friend and a singer with whom Kemo had sung till dawn in many cities, on the beaches of the Adriatic and in cafés, wherever they happened to be. A real Arsen letter, composed from the heart, with trepidation, with true love and sadness at the insanity that has propelled us back into the Stone Age.

With guitar and pen, Kemal Monteno wrote back to Arsen. He wrote a love song that keeps hovering over Sarajevo and over all of us. He wrote and sang about the things we were fully aware of, about exactly the same things that all of us here wanted to say but didn't know how to or didn't dare to. He did what he had promised himself to do. And he doesn't want to record it, nor will he allow anyone else to do so. If you are a Sarajevan, if you know what that means in this city now, and if you have the guts to be where on a cold night all real Sarajevans come, then perhaps you'll have a chance to hear it. But it has to be deep into the night, or at the crack of dawn, when you can be arrested because you're out after curfew and you might have to put up with the idea of continuing to dream in a warm room at the police station:

> *We got your letter,*
> *letter to a friend,*
> *lines of muffled hope.*
> *We write you back,*
> *our fingers numb*
> *on the surviving strings,*
> *while our hearts beat the rhythm,*
> *still pulsing*
> *to people blazing*
> *like a phoenix, like a phoenix,*
> *breathing the Sarajevo air*
> *pungent with the death of so much youth,*
> *my God, Dio mio . . .*

Then comes the part none of us, abandoned here to jackals in the name of "order" and "civilization," will ever forget. Words that cut us to the very marrow:

> *. . . we'll walk again*
> *along Daniel Ozmo Street,*
> *deep into the night, like we did,*
> *protected by the veil of friendship*
> *which always was and still is*
> *our very reason to live.*
> *For the first time I hope*
> *My God, Dio mio.*
> *We'll walk again*
> *along Haulikova Street*

just like we used to
and around the old bazaar,
woven with strands of friendship,
we'll stamp its footsteps
in the wet snow and on the cobblestones . . .
When you ask how we're doing
our only answer is
we're alive,
we're alive . . .

I don't know what else they can take away from Sarajevo to isolate it even further from the rest of the world. They've cut its telephone lines, destroyed its post office and killed its postmen, stopped its trains and knocked down its bridges, poisoned its carrier pigeons, and banned satellite connections. But still, the letter to Arsen went off to Zagreb, and much farther beyond. And it goes off every day, an infinite number of times.

We're alive. We're alive.

Santa Claus

". . . And my missing leg, the one they took away when I was hit by a shell, that happened here, in Sarajevo. Darko doesn't have a leg either, and Slaven doesn't have an arm. And Salem's puppy from our building lost a leg too. It just happens, what can you do? I'm the fastest with one leg, fastest of all in these three rooms. I could catch up with them even without a crutch.

"Who knows, maybe Santa Claus will bring me a leg for the new year. I'd sort of like that, if he can. If he can't, maybe it'll happen another time. . . ."

A six-year-old boy, at the hospital

A Little Love, Underground

Before the war Enver Dizdar was a journalist known to everybody in Sarajevo. Not because of his father [Mak Dizdar, the great Bosnian poet], but because of his own journalism. So it's not surprising that he stopped writing since, as he put it, this kind of "war" journalism made him sick. At one point a story was going around town about the question he had put, half in jest, to the doctors of Sarajevo: "Would it be possible to amputate the leg of a healthy cow and put an artificial one in its place? That way the starving people of Sarajevo would have something to eat and the cow could continue giving milk and producing calves . . ." Physicians, veterinarians and specialists in hospitals discussed the idea, which met with a mixed response, for days on end. The upshot of it all was that Enver decided he would never again even think of interfering in such "delicate" matters during the war. He then formed a little team of filmmakers to produce commissioned films, short documentaries and commercials, in order to survive. One of the stories he came upon as he was shooting around Sarajevo couldn't possibly fit into the format he was working with:

"I was in a French town called Fréjus once, during the Cannes Film Festival. I wasn't particularly impressed by Fréjus at the time. It neither seemed like a real town or a place on the coast. But my memory of Fréjus came back as I was making a film for a company of French soldiers serving with UNPROFOR. The company had come from Fréjus. That's how I met Jean-Paul Diuder, who was in charge of logistics. His mother was French and his father Algerian. Probably

55

because of that, he seemed to get what was going on around here better than a lot of other people. And he had a heart of gold. One day we went to the destroyed sports complex Zetra, where a poor refugee family had been living in the concrete cellar. They had moved because the French were fixing the place up to use as one of their bases, and all the 'civilians' had to go. I saw Diuder looking at a tearful fourteen-year-old girl, who reminded him of his daughter. The sight broke his heart. He did everything he could to keep them in that hovel, and he succeeded. After that he visited, fed, looked after, and comforted them. Secretly—because it wasn't legal—we managed to shoot a story about that family and their friendship with Diuder. The guys on our crew couldn't hide their tears during the shooting. I've never seen so much love and gratitude in one place. One day, Diuder left Sarajevo. The shells were coming down on the city like crazy, and I couldn't see him before his departure. So he didn't take a copy of the film about 'his family' along with him. I haven't been able to send it to him either. But I will take it to Fréjus one day, no matter what. He deserves it. First, I'll find my own kids in Germany and spend some time with them. Then I'll go to Fréjus. I owe it to him, that much is clear."

Who Is Crazy?

Fahro Memić is among those who defended *Oslobodenje* during the war, who saved both its good name and its life. His old friends say he's a man who functions best in absolutely abnormal, crazy times. That means that he functioned best throughout this war. He stood outside the newspaper building when it was on fire, just a few yards from the firefighter who was killed by a sniper while trying to do something against the raging flames. Later the same night, he helped his colleagues put the paper to bed. It came out, despite the rubble of the fire, to give Sarajevans new strength and hope. On the first days of the war he closed off all entrances to the abandoned *Oslbodenje* building with piles of paper and empty trucks, working only about a hundred yards from the front line. He showed up in every tough situation, in all the places only someone "crazy" could be found. Today, seven hundred days after the beginning of the war, he is where so many of other first fighters are: pushed aside to make room for the "new medal bearers" and "new heroes," those who were nowhere to be found when the fires blazed.

On the first "real" day of the war in Sarajevo, that bloody May 2, 1992, he was on Zrinski Street. Like thousands of other Sarajevans, he couldn't believe his eyes as he watched a gray-green self-propelled cannon "walk" into the city to get things ready for the worst, which was still to come. Everything was unexpected, confusing, shocking. Fighters of the Patriotic League of Bosnia and Herzegovina—a secret organization until then—showed up with mortars, rocket launchers and other weapons that Sarajevans had never seen before.

"It was unbelievable. I watched the cannon disappearing in flames, I saw the young men of the former People's Army get killed. My mind was teeming with questions: Why? For what? On whose behalf? It turned out later that the last question was the crucial one. On whose behalf?

"I started looking for Vesna. We were supposed to meet at Charly's but we didn't, it was too late. On all sides, insanity: by the cathedral, on Mejtas Hill, at the eternal-flame monument to the 1945 liberators of Sarajevo. I found Vesna at the café Lora, beside herself. 'Are these guys crazy?' she asked. I don't know. I only know that my city is under attack, that the target is everything I have ever had. And just then, as we were standing together in a passageway, the first 'real' grenade struck. A totally unknown, inconceivable sound, a crash, like the Earth's bowels turning inside out. A huge black wound opened up in Sarajevo's oldest department store on Tito Street. Everything is absolutely unreal, yet it's all happening in front of our own eyes. 'Are these people crazy? . . .' I look towards the Lisac café, where we had spent our youth. I keep thinking that if I run over there, I'll be able to sit down in peace like I used to, drink coffee, and talk to the owner as if nothing had happened. Then I called my office from somewhere. Busy. Then I called Radio Sarajevo. Milka Figurić answered. God, where could she be now? She put me right on the air, practically from the street. A direct broadcast of the killing of the city, of the killing of Bosnia-Herzegovina, of me, of my son Damir, my Željka, my Fahra, Nina . . . Are they really crazy?

"In the middle of a sentence—a new explosion. It hit a building next to the "eternal flame," above the Dekor store. I kept the telephone line open and ran over there to see what had happened. Then another explosion, right behind me. That's how the worst of it began, this killing that has been going on for seven hundred days now. I remember what Dobrica Ćosić, once a great writer and now a puny Serbian president, said to Radovan Karadžić at the beginning of the war: 'Everything has be done to make sure that whatever seemed impossible before becomes possible now.' A battle, literally, for our very lives, and for the life of *Oslobodenje*. A fight to remain on your feet for as long as you can.

"To this day the question Vesna asked me two years ago in May, 'Are these guys crazy?,' echoes in my ears.

"Yes, Vesna, they are, but we're even crazier. That's why we have survived."

Silly Kika

In happier times someone had coined a phrase that, despite its obvious sentimentality, really proved to be true: "Children are our greatest joy." Those who had and still have children long since grasped the full meaning of this piece of wisdom. "Children are the greatest tragedy of Sarajevo" has also become a truth that no one put quite this way before. But those with children in Sarajevo, as well as those without, have been living with this truth for months. And it's not just because of those kids who died from grenades or sniper bullets. The tragedy touches kids who missed the last train putting them on track to any kind of normal life, it includes tens of thousands of those who will be scarred forever by traumas and tics. Finally, it touches those who will embark upon life, nursed with hatred and intolerance. I listened to the father of a ten-year-old, who, with obvious pride, praised his son for ripping the maps of Serbia and Montenegro from the atlas. By doing this the boy had saved face, not only for his father but everyone around him. Tears of joy glistened in the eyes of the father, who "now knows that he has a real hero among his closest of kin."

Another guy, though, never uttered a word about this kind of paternal "heroism" to the children of Sarajevo, and those same children listened to him as if he were God himself, every Tuesday afternoon on the waves of Radio M. Just to add their amusement, he called himself Silly Kika. Or, to put it more precisely, "Silly Kika from Costa Rica," as he introduced his wild show because "small guys don't like trouble." For the dying kids of Sarajevo, Kika is the childhood that has been taken away from them by force, a brother and friend, a neighbor and a legendary hero, Santa Claus and Superman, the Ninja Turtle, and the father lost, God only knows where. Kids believe in Silly Kika more than war and peace; five-year-old girls confide in him their greatest heartthrobs and deepest secrets. It is from him and no one else that kids who don't even have bread can get a cookie and the hope that, as sure as eggs are eggs, there'll be more cookies again one day, more than you can even imagine.

Sarajevo's incredible guy, Silly Kika, visits hospitals every day to see his little buddies, with a bagful of cookies and candy. God only knows where he gets such things. With a real goatee and a shaven head, he used to be kind of stout, but now he's just a shadow of his former self with eternal smile on his lips. Kika probably isn't exactly the kind of guy that normal kids out there in the world would find too appealing. But the kids in Sarajevo are not normal. They are abnormally normal, so it is abnormally very important to have Silly Kika around to talk to every Tuesday afternoon at the same time if they can get a phone line. If not, they write or somehow get a message to Radio M that they called but couldn't get through, and Kika will for sure, absolutely for sure, call them before the next show and ask them what it is they need.

"Kika, Kika, do you know who's calling?"

"I know, it's Nina. Nina, sweetheart, do you have any problems?"

"No, Kika, I don't. Yesterday, my friends came to visit, we celebrated my fourth birthday. Do you want me to tell you a joke that I heard yesterday, Kika?"

"Yes, Nina, yes of course my horse."

"OK, here it goes. Suljo comes to visit Mujo and finds him on the balcony rocking himself in a rocking chair. 'What on earth are you doing out there?' asks Suljo. 'I'm giving the snipers a hard time,' answers Mujo. Isn't that a good one, Kika?"

"Brilliant, Kika's honey. Which would you like better: a cake or a free haircut at Auntie Rada's? A haircut, of course, that's what I thought. Today in our city, the most important thing is to be beautiful. We have to screw up those bad guys out there with our beauty, don't you think? And you know the easiest way you can become beautiful? Just say to yourself: I want to be beautiful, I *can* be beautiful, and that's it. Little kids don't like trouble . . . Silly Kika from Costa Rica loves you. . . ."

I Am Sad

Nine-year-old Lejla Kalajdžić lives in Sarajevo, in the center of the city, with thousands of other children. At her neighbors' house she saw a letter that their kids, refugees in Germany, wrote to them. They are about the same age as Lejla. After she read it, Lejla took a sheet of paper and wrote back to Germany—kind of a reply to their letter that, even though it wasn't written to her, could just as well have been.

She wrote:

"Dear Bor and Gorcin,

I saw your photographs. I like you. I am a neighbor of your parents. I read your letter and saw how you spend your days. Now I am going to describe my typical day to you. I get up early and go to get bread for my family and my neighbors. We can buy bread from seven to eight in the morning. After that we can't, it's all gone. I am scared because shells keep falling and snipers keep shooting. That is the only time I go out. The rest of the time I stay home. I don't go to school because there is no electricity or heat. I study on my own but without books or notebooks. We get electricity once a month and then watch television. I have no friends because there are no other children in our house and I am not supposed to go out. I am sad.

You have it good. You have something to eat. You go skating. You have streetlights. Only you don't have your parents there. They are nice. I have it good too because I love your parents and they're happy you're alive, that you go to school and you're well. With many greetings, I hope to see you sometime.

Your friend,

Lejla"

Stretching the Brain

If we still followed Sarajevo's pre–World–War II trends in fashion, when gentlemen wore Girardi hats [a flat and hard straw hat named after the Austrian actor Alexandre Girardi], gaiters covering part of their shoes, and carried canes topped with ivory knobs, Zoran Bečić would certainly fit the bill. A gentleman from head to toe, as the old ladies would say with a sigh. Upright, always smiling, he looks you straight in the eye, neither to the right nor left. It's hard to tell whether he's like that because he can't get rid of the stage in him when he's *not* acting—a profession in which he reached the top—or whether he owes his theatrical success to the fact that he is simply a born comedian.

Today, it's theater again. Even though he's gotten so skinny, his eyes sunken, quieter than before. In the remarkable atmosphere of his old elegant apartment in the ruined heart of town, he opened a "place," just for friends. No one can bring themselves to utter the obvious word *café*. They can't, because Zoran doesn't really run a "café." For a café, you need someone in control, the owner-businessman or the owner-bouncer. A wheeler-dealer. Zoran is none of those things; he is simply an elegant man in an old, luxurious apartment. There, he entertains friends and visitors by an exquisitely crafted model sailboat, among beautiful pieces he gathered from travels around the world, among paintings quite unlike those usually found in cafés. Like on stage in who knows what play from "those" days, Zoran pushes a cart with drinks on it and asks you what you would like. It's hard to believe he isn't on stage. Only sometimes, as if from far away, he smiles when he hears a knock on the door to his "place." Whoever heard of knocking on the door of a café? Even so, he is glad people knock, because that way—even subconsciously— he knows they don't treat his place like a café. Especially not in this war, if you can call it a war.

"That horrible night in May of 1992, when Mladić was tearing Sarajevo apart, he said something unbelievable to his commanders as they pulled the triggers on howitzers and rocket launchers. 'Stretch their brains,' he said. Remember that? Back then, even when I listened to a recording of that command, I couldn't possibly figure out what he meant. I think that today, almost two years later, I understand what he had in mind, what he meant to do, and what he finally did. The other day I went out of my house to go to the theater and act in a play. I knew my part very well. I always like to memorize my parts thoroughly. And you know what happened? On the way to the theater, I realized that I didn't even know what play I was going to act in. I couldn't remember its title, its author, or who else was playing in it. I knew the part, but I didn't know where it came from. I couldn't believe it myself. What was going on with me? I was caught in the fear of madness and the misery that goes with it. It was only later, long after that, that I calmed down and convinced myself it was a crazy, passing incident, that it happened to everybody starved of vitamins and calories—you know our stupid theories about diets.

"Then it caught up with me again. After five months in which I had no contact with my daughter, a man who came here to see me offered to arrange an international phone call so I could talk to her. I don't know how he managed to get that connection, or where he works. I went nuts from happiness. After so much time, we finally got to talk. The following day the man came over again. He was glad that I managed to talk with my daughter, and I was about to tell him how the conversation went. I couldn't remember anything. Not one single word, one thought, absolutely nothing. Now, I have finally begun to understand what Mladić meant when he said to his commanders: 'Stretch their brains!' There is nothing here any more, no memories, nothing to remember, and nothing to hope for. And every time I think we've reached rock bottom, that it's the limit, that it couldn't be any worse, a new layer opens up, a new chasm, a new dimension of pain and suffering. And you can even go beyond that, into a still deeper, darker, and more horrifying abyss. The worst thing is that we have suffered and survived all that. I hate survival, and I'm desperate because of it."

Fire

"... There was nothing left to make fire with. We'd already torn apart everything we could—carpets, mats, old shoes and nightgowns, pants and sweaters. The saddest moments were when the fire swallowed up the glossy pages of old fashion magazines. My friend and I looked at the impeccably made-up, thin and tanned models happily smiling back at us. We caught ourselves staring at gourmet ads for smoked ham and mushrooms, cheeses, even garnished potatoes. In sadness and anger, longing and resignation, we stuffed all those pictures that had been such a mundane part of our life but are now an unreal and unreachable dream into our small handmade stove.

"The books came last. We always had a special relationship with books. Maybe not like all the highbrows who really overdo it when they talk about books. I don't even know exactly why, but books were unconsciously pushed aside, behind carpets and clothing, and we thought their turn would only come at the bitter end. They lasted a long time because the winter was pretty mild. But then, we had no choice: in went *Her Mother's Sin* by Miriam, a popular romance writer, then *Everything About Beauty*, then *Home Cookbook*, which we never needed anyway, then Yugoslav and foreign revolutionaries, various biographies and autobiographies, 'revolutionary' and 'counterrevolutionary' works.

"One morning I laid my hand on a book by Vladimir Dedijer, who used to be an official Communist Party historian. I can't remember the title. I know we were cold and wanted to make ourselves the little bit of coffee we had gotten from somewhere. Just to warm up. As I started to tear the first pages out, our neighbor Danka showed up at the door. She was an older woman who came to our place a lot. She always managed to figure out exactly what was going on in the house right away: who was or had been there, what was new in the kitchen or in the pot. Her first glance caught the pages of the book disappearing into the fire. Seeing the name of the author and the title, she asked loudly, ironically, enunciating every syllable of her question, 'Are you burning it because he's a Serb?'

'You know what Auntie Danka, I would burn it if my own father had written it. There, just like that—if my Rudo had written it, it would go right into the fire today.'

'Come on now, by God, don't burn that book, give it to me, I'll save it.'

'We'll give it you if you can bring us some wood instead of the book. We have to burn something and this is all we have left.'

"Then she went away. A little later, she showed up at the door with several long bars of wood, two or three inches wide, nicely trimmed and painted. They all had the same number, 1994, inscribed on them. One still clearly showed: 1971–1994. There was no dilemma. Not even a week ago, these had been crosses in a nearby cemetery. Crosses from graves of people buried there only a few days ago, since 1994 had just begun. The sign of the last resting place of a Sarajevan only twenty-three years old. We all know how and why twenty-three-year-olds depart this life, here in Sarajevo.

'Auntie Danka, my God, this is from the graves . . .'

'What can you do, my child, you must do something to live through all this.'

"We didn't want anything else from Dedijer except to help us get through all this. But Auntie Danka said, 'That's not the same . . .' The book is still with her, and will remain with her until the last cross."

Maria Tolj, who told this story, is of Croatian origin. She and her Serb friend Mira have been in Sarajevo throughout the war, by their own choice. They came early on from their family's homes on the other side of Sarajevo's encirclement "to be with friends." At the end of January, when we had our first real snowstorm, they were burning pieces of an old wardrobe from the patio. Those days, it was really warm in their house.

A Ruse

"They had been staking out my house for days, thinking, I guess, that I would hide when they brought me the order to go to the trenches. I must admit that I enjoyed secretly watching them as they plotted a way to get me. I had a slip of paper in my pocket that said they couldn't take me away. You should have seen the dumbfounded look on their faces when they caught me and I put the slip under their noses. I knew that next time they would think of a trick to get me to go, at least for one shift. Then I thought of a ruse.

"They had come and taken me away with some new papers that were OK, and I couldn't do anything about it. They told me to take a three-day shift and if there wasn't any shooting that I'd make out like a bandit. And there wasn't, I just crouched in the trench by the wall of some cemetery, and I was happy as hell that I'd taken them for a ride. They thought they could screw around with me. Know what I did? I wrote *six* poems! You know what that means? Six poems! You know how long it usually takes me to write six poems? Two months, at least."

One of the poems that Dragan Martinović, economist, designer, waiter and poet, wrote in a trench by a cemetery goes like this:

> *Real rats usually start wars*
> *when the rabble's had their fill.*
> *What do all the victories mean to me*
> *when I'm about to go down in defeat.*
> *The disease came down on me from Pale,*

I'm utterly done in every which way I go.
So it's good to lose another battle, everything
worth anything's just gone down the tubes.
The mad embrace the perplexed,
and once again, evil carries the day.
Because I'm sure of it,
every bullet is a hit.
I'm even scared of my own shadow
and everything that's happening to me.
Anyone who's normal now is scared to death,
even though it's all the same to idiots.
Everything around us is filthy,
even though it should be clean . . .

A few days later, Dragan went off to see some petty bureaucrat in charge of financial support for "cultural workers." He went to prove himself, and look into whether any "humanitarian aid" might be coming his way. The petty bureaucrat just gave him a dirty look, and full of self-importance, told him: "Sure, while heroes are dying on the front, you're writing poetry."

"I didn't know that Vladimir Nazor [famous poet who joined the Partisans fighting the Nazis in World War II] was a war criminal and a profiteer," said Dragan, more to himself, and walked out.

Two days later, he was back in the trenches, very near the graveyard.

Dragan Martinović, a poet, among other things

Where the President
Does Not Live

On King Tomislav Street—the name honors a Croatian king so it's at risk of being changed by the newly "faithful"—there is a hairdresser's salon called DM, owned by Muhamed Dedajić, men's hair stylist or just plain barber, to use the more popular Sarajevan term. Contrary to the logic of either urban design or local aesthetics, the large front double door of the salon is painted red, and can be seen from the surrounding hills. It is the only door on the street whose name still waves like a precarious banner in the winds of the newly zealous nationalists; it has stayed open throughout the war ready to serve the young and old, soldiers and civilians, the loaded and the broke, those eager to hear the latest news or just gossip. It's even open to the reticent, those who only listen and frown without saying a word. Actually—and Muhamed himself would even attest to this—the place was closed only once, when Sarajevo saved face by fighting against the rulers of the mafia, the infamous Caco and his buddy Ćelo.

"Why did I come here every day? How should I know? What else could I do? Everybody seemed to be looking to see if my door would open or not. If it opened, others came too. My neighbor Zijo, a shoemaker, and I have been like barometers. Another neighbor told me a hundred times: 'You know, Muhamed, when you're late, I somehow get cold around my heart. I keep thinking, it's all finished. . . .' And there are other reasons why I'm in the shop every day. Often, young men with rifles and automatics come in and say, 'Come on, Muhamed, give us a haircut and a shave. Tonight we're going to fight at Kromolj, or on Zlatište, or on Poljine, and we want to look nice and neat.' And they all laugh and kid around with me.

"I also have to be here when my friend Avdo from the waterworks comes by. He always checks to see if everything's all right with me. In the beginning the two of us used to come here together, because his office is near by. We would go through that park up over there by Ciglane—you know, I mean where the park *used* to be—while they were blasting from all sides. Sometimes there'd be an explosion close by and we'd dive into the grass in style, like real goalies. Then Avdo would get up and say: 'That was pretty cool, man. Save!' Or still smiling, even with the shrapnel all around us, Avdo would rebuke me: 'That save was no good—look what a mess you made out of yourself.' And so it's been going on for months. How much longer? I have no idea. Maybe until the day when my friend Zdravko Grebo and I can do what we promised each other at the very beginning of the war—get out of Sarajevo for a short trip, a place we can get enough sleep, and eat and drink something good. But it has to be a place we can get to by train, as regular passengers, with real tickets from the station. In any direction. Until then, it's war for us, and haircuts for the army and everyone else."

That's why the red door on "the street President Izetbegović no longer lives on" stays wide open. That, in fact, is how Muhamed the barber described the address of his salon in a commercial on Zdravko's radio show. At the beginning of the war the president lived only about a dozen houses down on King Tomislav Street. Then he moved. Everybody's been guessing why ever since. Muhamed doesn't go into it. He won't comment. But maybe his ad said it all.

A Terrific Guy

Before the war, in the days of dull, slow, conventional news photographers, they called him Lightning. No need to explain why. He was always one step ahead of everyone, always in the right place at the right time, before anyone else got there.

In the war he got the moniker Terrific. Again, there's no need to explain why. He put on a show of pictures of Tito, all the pictures that had been taken down, broken, ripped or saved, wrapped and framed again, everything he found wandering through the ruins of the city, places no one else dared to venture. The show went up at the Skenderija arena, impossible to get to at the time without putting your life on the line or your face under the crosshairs of a sniper's sight fixed on you from one of the surrounding hills.

He used to say, with a smile, "Whoever doesn't have the guts to run across the bridge at Skenderija shouldn't even see the show at all." But many did run across the bridge. The lighting was strictly by candle, but the show stayed up a long time. Later on, you had to bring your own candle if you wanted to see the photos. And a lot of people did. Terrific joked again, in his own quiet way: "Now it turns out, I've done a performance piece: running, snipers, candles, and Tito. I'll be damned if it isn't."

Milomir Kovačević, Mr. Terrific, Lightning, is a man who can't get out of his huge den—that great apartment that six people used to live in, occupied only by himself now—without someone stopping him to ask, "How about my picture?" "It'll be done," he says, and it does get done. It seems that the only guy who didn't ask him for a picture was that huge dinosaur whose plaster head, taken from the destroyed museum, is now in his "den." "He didn't get a chance," says Terrific, "we ate him before he found his way around our house. Can't you smell smoked meat everywhere around here?" And it smells of burning. There was a fire in the neighborhood. Now, you can hear the sound of a trumpet coming from there. A trumpeter moved in who practices all day long. "He's the only one I haven't taken a picture of. But his turn will come, we can't forget him. If we do, all these people will be forgotten one day, and those who hightailed it out of here during the first days of the war will plant their butts back in here to take control again and rent out our memories. I want, at least for myself, the faces of all the poor people who were here when it mattered to be here. Who knows, it might even come in handy. . . ."

As for the story, there isn't one, only the pictures, if anyone's interested.

Perfume for the American Lady

Whoever lives in the center of Sarajevo and doesn't know where the Bisera boutique was before the war, or where the café bearing the same name is today, knows nothing about downtown Sarajevo or who Sarajevans really are, and could only arouse suspicion among the locals as to his or her right to be called a Sarajevan. Not because Bisera is so different from all those that make Sarajevo the city it is, but for precisely the opposite reason: she epitomizes everything Sarajevo is to such an extent it is absolutely impossible *not* to know her. For years now, men have turned to look at her with a sigh of desire. Even so, the changes she's gone through have been subtle to the point of being provocative: her gradually increasing smiles, another bracelet, yet another ring on her fingers, one more golden pendant. But she has always been ready, more than anyone else downtown, to come to the aid of poor people whom life has denied one thing or another.

I know some people who've already started betting on how long Bisera will last with her "big mouth," which takes obvious pleasure in going over events everybody knows of but doesn't want to talk about. Maybe that's why, from the beginning of the war to this day, all kinds of people in uniforms with shiny insignias come to her café for drinks. Even those who found themselves, to their great surprise, in positions of power, show up hoping to hear—even if only through a joke—the latest gossip about themselves. More than a few wish they had never come.

Bisera once asked me if I thought she should let in "the show-offs from CNN" who planned to shoot a story about Sarajevo's women; they planned to show how women go about their mornings and prepare for work. I told her she should, by all means, because if she didn't someone else would and that would be another story altogether. A few days later I dropped by the café and heard the following story:

"They came earlier than they said they would. Cameramen, technicians, gofers, translators, and some rich lady, a middle-aged reporter. You know me: corset, long low-necked togs, then the bathroom, cosmetics, the little towels carefully sorted by shade and size. What do they think, that we are poor and primitive? They just stared when I started with my masks, powders and perfumes. All from old stocks, of course, but I happened to have everything I needed. Then I asked them if they would like some whiskey with their coffee, some rolls and the rest. Since they were so amazed about everything, my spiteful streak got the better of me: it was clear to me they thought no one else had a right to Revlon, Chanel, or Cartier, or anything else, for that matter. Why, I could see them asking themselves, was I born with such things here in Sarajevo, in my mother's house who, by the way, was also quite a lady. You know what they asked me when I got the jewelry out of the box? Did I get all that in the war? If only they knew about all the things I sold to give some money to the soldiers and the poor in this war. And when I was done dressing and got my fur coat from the hanger, I just couldn't restrain myself: I was watching the American lady, still puzzled about my perfumes. You know what I did? I took the best one and gave it to her. What does it matter? It will make her happy and it won't make a damn bit of difference to me. I'll find another one whenever I need it."

The Leo News

In Sarajevo, you need say no more than "Kula," no further explanation is needed. What else and who else could it be but Kula. Before the war he was an electrical engineer, computer and cybernetics expert, father of a son, Jan-Zlatan, an eternal traveler, and a great jester. Today he is legendary; a trench digger at Žuć, the city's most famous defense line, vendor of all kinds of newspapers, and the sole publisher, writer and radio-reader of his own paper, *The Leo News*. Unlike other newspapers, it is handwritten in one, two, or three copies, and can be read in the center of town, on the door of an old house on Hasan Kikić Street, tucked under the eaves, just enough so the paper can survive the first rain or snow. *The Leo News*—a miracle in the beginning, today it is essential nourishment for the souls of Sarajevans. Malik Kulenović, author, editor, and publisher, once just a citizen, the guy next door, today—Kula. A phenomenal man, a legendary man, a real person.

Kula's newspaper featured this item the other day:

"Something you see every day. Cane in hand, an old man flips boxes and digs through a garbage container. His dog, even though he is unable to rise to the occasion because of his size, doesn't lose his enthusiasm even after ten unsucessful attempts to jump into the container. With his little tail, he tries to make the old man aware of his presence. Hunger, illiteracy, or something else prevented them from reading a warning notice: 'Do not litter! Whatever there was to eat, we have eaten! Whatever there was to burn, we have burned! Thank you for your concern about the environment!' Signed: Tenants of the Apartment Building, Entrance 15.

What is not part of the everyday picture is the photographs, the ripped-up albums scattered everywhere, out in the open, for all to see: 'Foto-Rekord' from 1939, a family, framed in a typical pose; 'Foto-Daskal,' Makarska, 1964, donkey and grandfather with granddaughter. That's what it looks like. A lady passing by picks a picture up from the ground and, carefully, somehow with affection, wipes the dust from it. 'Do you know them?' someone else asks. 'No, but I can't help thinking to myself, my God, who has *my* pictures from my apartment in Grbavica, now that they control it? I left the house in a raincoat and slippers; I didn't even take my albums. Where on earth are all these people now?'

Yes, where indeed are the people in that picture now?

Everyone forgot about the old man, the dog, their work and even their trench for a second. In less then ten minutes, all the photos were in a box and the box was carefully placed against the door to Entrance 15.

Let's not throw away our memories. Don't let the past disappear in fire. In the name of the future.

At the end of the text, it says: "From albums and containers."

These days Kula has also written a few new aphorisms, for us and his paper. Everybody likes this one: "It's time for solidarity—Let's help Europe!"

The Thread of Life

Vlado Mrkić is someone I had never really had a serious drink with, one on one, or shared a big story with, yet I always considered him a good friend. I was sure he would do anything for me just as I would for him; nor would he have to explain why or have the patience to listen to unnecessary and meaningless stories of valor so typical of some people.

I remember when, back in the hot summer of 1992, he was the only one—literally the only one—with the will and courage to get into a beat-up Golf and tear through the streets of Sarajevo, (torn apart from one end to the other by shells, bombs, explosions, and bullets of all calibers), to bring the rest of us, trapped in the *Oslobodenje* building, texts from which we made the newspaper. Then he would come again at the crack of dawn in the very same Golf to pick up freshly printed papers and, racing across parts of the city only a madman would consider passable, take them to friends who sold them in the center of town.

Even in better days, he didn't say much. Once, a long time ago, while working as a correspondent for *Oslobodenje* in Cairo, I "took him off the plane" on his way to Ethiopia, to have him stay with me for a few days so that he could see at least a little bit of Egypt. At various evening affairs, he listened to the same old story gone over ad infinitum by people from the Yugoslav Embassy, by directors of branch offices of Yugoslav companies and others who worked in Cairo: how and where to invest their money when they return to Yugoslavia, how high the interest rates are here and there, how they can get a better return for their money. He only listened and kept quiet. One night, in the heat of these calculations, a man loaded with money asked him, "Excuse me, you're coming from our country, how do they calculate interest in our banks on a six-month time deposit?" "I don't have a clue," said Vlado, "I'm not interested in what I don't have. Since you have money you ought to know such questions shouldn't be addressed to people who don't." I remember the party breaking up in silence soon after that. Even after Vlado left for Ethiopia and went back to Sarajevo nobody discussed money, investments, profits, or interest rates anymore.

Once, on the eve of the war in Bosnia and Herzegovina, Vlado broke up another party in almost the same way. This time it was a party of journalists. As one of the very few who moved around former Yugoslavia visiting places where the seams of the happy country were being ripped, as a true witness of the bloody dramas at Vukovar, Kozarac, Petrovo Selo, Ravno, and so many other places, he was awarded *Oslobodenje*'s annual prize for outstanding journalism. But at the ceremony, right when most of the guests already had a drink in one hand and meat on a fork or toothpick in the other, someone brought a brief letter from the laureate for the chairman of the jury. It read:

"Nobody ever asked for my permission to give me this or any other award for my stories published in *Oslobodenje*. You have no right to do that. I didn't run around Yugoslavia chasing after misery, witnessing the suffering, the blood, and the hate in order to be awarded prizes and money for it. So much from me. Greetings, Vlado Mrkić."

"Something simply drew me to places where things were happening. You know, it's been that way since the beginning, since the events in Kosovo. I'll never forget our driver, Zdravko, that night when we saw for the first time a column of tanks from the former Yugoslav People's Army heading south. Zdravko drove silently through the night past the column, as a tear rolled down his face. He couldn't understand what was happening to us, who was going to fight who, and why, after all these years. That's the way it was with me too. I didn't do it because I had to, not even later when I was on my own because Zdravko and the others refused to drive. I knew that somewhere in the newsroom, editors were sitting around drinking whiskey, while I was putting my life on the line. I knew a lot of people were saying I was crazy. I remember my wife asking me a hundred times, 'How much longer, Vlado? You've done enough. Why doesn't someone else go?' But even so, I couldn't give up. I'd do the same today. They can keep the awards for those whose turn it is, who've already been 'chosen.' That's the way it's always been."

In his book *Never Again Together*, a collection of reports published in *Oslobodenje* from the days the smell of gunpowder began to spread throughout Yugoslavia until the middle of 1993, he put together a series of poignant stories which he concluded by saying: "The last hope that this war might end soon has been extinguished; it will last for a long time, because it lasts longest when they are killing your soul."

One of the stories is called "The Thread of Life." It is about a woman who was to give birth on a day many considered the worst in Sarajevo throughout the whole war. He tells about bringing the woman to the emergency clinic and then having to leave her there because it was impossible to get to the hospital. He didn't even know her name.

"... My chance acquaintance stayed in the corner of the waiting room at the emergency clinic with only a small bag in her lap. I just said 'good luck,' as she whispered, more to herself than to me 'Maybe we'll see each other again some time.'

A few days later I heard she had given birth to a son. I know nothing more about her—where she is now, what her name is—

nothing. I only know that after that encounter I somehow felt better in my soul.

I know that woman, who, with so much joy, went to deliver another human being into the world on that hellish day of war, is the thread of life that no war can snap."

In mid-January 1994, I met Vlado on the street. Kind of stooped over, he looked dark and a bit sad. I didn't want to ask him what was the matter, because such questions are entirely superfluous these days in Sarajevo. You simply don't ask. If someone has something to tell you, they will. And Vlado told me: In a small, second-rate paper that sprang up somewhere in Sarajevo, a man who calls himself President of the Association of Journalists wrote a piece about fifth-column journalists and put Vlado's name on the list. I know why. Because Vlado is a Serb and there is no room for people of his kind in the heads of the newfangled patriots. Because such "new heroes" are just the other side of the coin of those on the hills who are destroying Sarajevo and about whom Vlado has written more real news items than all those so called "heroes" put together.

The difference between those "patriots" and Vlado precisely corresponds to the number of times my reticent friend got in his car to take stories and papers from one end of the city to the other. He even managed to write a few, back when very few did. Not to mention bringing a woman to a clinic in his own arms, "the thread of life." How many feats of true courage the pathetic, failed "geniuses" of this war actually carried out, we shall never know.

"You know, as long as thirty years ago a friend of mine from school used to tell me we'd be at each other's throats one day. He was saying that thirty years ago and I still can't believe it, not even after the worst has happened, after seeing everything with my own eyes. And you know what else? While I was saying that the worst wouldn't happen, my reports told a different story. You could see the evil coming. It was as if I didn't believe my own stories. As if they, too, had betrayed me. And they were right, those stories, not me. That's what's so terrible.

I did all this not because I had to, but because I wanted to. Because that's the way I am. And you know what? I'd do it all over again. And I'm glad that's the way it is, I'm glad we're not all the same."

The Cat

"One day this winter a mouse showed up in my mother's house, just like so many other houses in Sarajevo. First one, then another, then a whole family. There was panic in the house, even though I could never understand why people were afraid of those cute little creatures. I even remember that, as a little girl, I secretly fed them until I was discovered. It didn't end well, neither for me nor the mice. This time, though, the situation was more serious: the smart mice of Sarajevo don't react to glue or the poisoned grain sold on the street for five marks. Things being the way they are, my mother said the only logical thing to do is get a cat, because cats must also be hungry in this misery. So she went to her sister's, whose daughter had a rather belligerent cat, to try and persuade my little cousin to lend us her cat for a few days. Her response was, actually, rather unexpected: in spite of all the effort at persuasion, the little girl wouldn't even hear of 'lending' her cat for such dirty business. Finally, on her way back, in the hallway of the building, my mother saw a beautiful black-and-white cat. Obviously receptive to loving care, he didn't resist at all as my mother put him in her bag.

"The problems started when she got home with the cat. The purported mouse hunter showed absolutely no interest in crouching in front of the hole from where a little gray mouse appeared now and then. He stretched lazily on the armchair next to the fire and didn't move a hair when a bowl of milk was put in front of him. Can you imagine: milk for a cat in Sarajevo! Half an hour later my mother put out a piece of meat for him from a can we had gotten the day before in a food package sent from abroad God knows when. That didn't interest him the least little bit either. It was quite clear that the cat belonged to a circle of Sarajevans who weren't exactly dying of hunger.

"As we thought over what to do, the phone rang. It was my aunt. She lost no time asking 'How's the cat you took yesterday? . . . Yeah, black and white, and fat . . . You've really done it this time: you've taken our prime minister's cat. Everyone's in a panic. They're looking for him everywhere, and some kids told them you'd taken away a cat just like theirs. Bring him back right away, for God's sake.'

"I burst out laughing. We must have been pretty swift to think the prime minster's cat would catch mice. We are, of course, dealing with an antigenocidal cat, one that cannot behave like an agressor. Also, one that doesn't drink powdered milk or eat meat from a can. Not to mention stale bread and rice. After all, where the prime minister's cat is, mice can really play.

"We took the cat quickly back to where my mom had found him and came back home to continue life with our little mice."

Amra Zulfikarpašić, painter and designer

Funeral

"A friend of mine had died and I missed his funeral. I didn't know where and when he was to be buried. A little later, another friend was killed. We had spent our lives together. The day he was killed by a shell fired from a hill, we had been together half an hour earlier. When I arrived at the graveyard where he was buried, it was already too late. A similar thing happened to my friend Tvrtko Kulenović, a writer. He arrived at the cemetery when his wife's grave was already filled in. All this happens because no one dares to inform the friends, neighbors, and relatives of the dead where and when their loved ones are to be buried.

"Over fifty Sarajevans were killed by shells or sniper bullets at funerals in Sarajevo's makeshift cemeteries. In the Lion Cemetery alone, ten gravediggers were killed while performing burials. No wonder we don't have proper funerals any more, just a mad rush to fill the hole with earth, so people can leave as fast as possible from those cursed places that are constantly targeted by those on the hills. That's why the death notices in newspapers have that absurd and totally senseless wording: 'The burial will take place at the scheduled time and location.' That's how far we've come. They torture us, they kill us, and in the end they won't even give us a moment to bid our dead a dignified farewell. That's unheard of anywhere in the world. Even the law of the jungle is more lenient.

"Who are those people? What are they like? Does it ever occur to them that they, too, will have to bury their own one day? If at least mothers had a right to bid farewell to their sons one last time. What kind of 'university professor' and 'Shakespearean scholar' is this Mr. Koljević, presumably the second from the top of their 'Serb Republic'? How come he never mustered enough strength, in the name of that 'Shakespearean scholarship' of his, to tell the thugs around him not to shoot at cemeteries and kill people at funerals? Disrespect for the dead is much worse than hatred for the living. It's the last line dividing us from animals. Beyond that, there's nothing else."

Fuko Hadžihalilović, Director of Collegium Artisticum

The Gas Pistol
and Other Weapons

"For years before the war I had a friend called Fadil, who lived in a village near Gračanica, near Tuzla. I remember him often these past months, especially when I listen to the news and realize I don't want to hear anything bad, that I want them to lie to me, to make a fool out of me, as long as they tell me something nice.

"A little before the war, Fadil asked me to lend him a book of old heroic ballads, saying, 'Please, just don't bring me those that say we're losing, I only want the ones where we win. Man, I really don't like it when we don't win.' So he made his children, way out there far from any city, read him heroic epics every night. If one of them happened to forget his father's warning and recited just a few lines in which 'our side' was losing, the poor kid would go to bed with his cheeks burning. Observing things in his village, though, Fadil knew what was going on, what was being said, and what was in the offing.

"Right on the eve of the war, I saw Fadil again. This time he asked me very seriously, 'Tell me, are you people in Sarajevo buying any weapons?'

'Here and there, but not much.'

'And what about you, do you have anything?'

'What do you mean do I have anything? What should I have?'

'Have you got a pistol, a rifle, a machine gun?'

'I don't.'

'And do you have five hundred marks?'

'I do.'

'Then you're crazy. How can you have five hundred marks and no arms at home. God save you, man.'

"So I went home remembering for the first time that I had some kind of a tear-gas gun, for scaring people off, something a bullet had never passed through. Hiding from my wife, I went looking for it. When I found it, I started looking it over and fooling around with it, set on taking one of the six cartridges out of the chamber. 'Playing' around like that, I fired it off by accident and all hell broke loose. My wife came running into the room frantically, thinking I had done something serious. There was smoke and tear gas all over the place. Everyone was in a panic. The neighbors came running in, but I didn't know what to tell them. The only thing that came to my mind at the time was: 'My, my, Pujdo, what shitty soldiers we are. What would Fadil say to this?'

"The next day I left the gun deep in a drawer, under some linen, so I would never see it again. Fadil made it to Sarajevo a few months later to 'take care of some business and get back to his peaceful village as soon as possible.' "

"What do you mean 'peaceful'? " I asked, flabbergasted. I knew that battles were raging around Gračanica.

'Just as I said, my friend. In our village, we were completely ready for the war before it started. We had as many rifles, bombs, and machine guns as we needed. Each house had something. When some hooligans came to attack the village, every burst of fire was met by us, every bomb of theirs was met by one of ours. So they just packed up and left. That's what you call "balance of power." You have nobody else to blame but yourselves. Didn't I tell you what to do before the war?'

"Of course, I didn't dare tell him the story of my gas pistol and our "fighting ability." Five hundred marks! I'd have given ten thousand if I'd had it just so they wouldn't push one of those devices into my hand. But now I think to myself: Fadil is right—we have no one to blame but ourselves."

Mustafa Mustafić (Pujdo), cameraman

Fire and Tears

"A long time ago, on May 18, 1978, our small group of journalists from Sarajevo attended the meeting of the International Olympic Committee in Athens. They were making the decision about who would host the next Winter Olympic Games, the fourteenth. It boiled down to three candidates: Saporo in Japan, Göteborg in Sweden, or Sarajevo in Bosnia and Herzegovina. The likely favorites, the Swedes and the Japanese, were self-confident and relaxed, while we were quiet and a little scared.

"Lord Killanin, president of the IOC, came out to the steps of the building where the meeting had taken place. He knew what the decision was. Other members of the Olympic Committee hadn't yet been informed, according to the new regulations. The Lord announced the best news we could have imagined: Sarajevo would host the fourteenth Winter Olympic Games in 1984. Three hundred journalists from all over the world had covered the meeting and, naturally, all the telephone booths at the Athens' Hotel Karavel were immediately occupied. Both the Japanese and the Swedes had open lines with their editorial offices, while I, as a reporter for Radio Sarajevo, had to win the favors of an operator in the Athens Post Office by being especially nice to her for our whole stay. At least this helped me get a connection to Sarajevo before my turn. My call was taken by Rinko Golubović, an announcer. Quite beside myself with excitement, I asked him to interrupt the program at what was just before two P.M. so I could announce the historical piece of news. Radio Sarajevo had never before interrupted its program and, of course, Rinko had to consult with the then editor-in-chief Ivica Mišić. Ivica agreed, they played the station's jingle—a stylized version of 'Tito Is Crossing Romanija'—and the listeners must have thought that something horrible had happened, something like a war. Instead, it was me announcing that Sarajevo had just been approved as the host of the Olympic Games. Like a flash of lightning, the news raced through the city, its restaurants and cafés, houses and trollies, everybody was blowing horns, singing, exclaiming their joy. Sarajevo quickly became a huge construction site, heavy machinery started roaring on the surrounding hills. On the mountains of Jahorina, Bjelašnica, and Igman new roads were built, new sports facilities, new hotels ... Everyone knows how Sarajevo organized those Games. It was a veritable fable on snow and ice. As people said, they were the best organized Games in the history of the Olympics, a fitting expression of what is most beautiful in the Olympic idea itself. In Sarajevo, like few Games before or after, there were no boycotts. Everybody who cared about sport was there: the Americans with their friends and allies, the Soviets with 'theirs.' Sarajevo was, indeed, above politics and divisions of any kind.

"But now our city is being destroyed and torn apart. One day I saw myself turned into a war reporter and, in that new role, my saddest mission was to report on the fire in the large Olympic sports center, Zetra. I found myself among the firefighters who tried to put out the flames engulfing the magnificent arena hit by incendiary rockets from the hills. The fire engines got there right away, but the big problem was water. What they had in the tanks was quickly used up, and when they switched to hydrants it became clear that wouldn't work either: there wasn't enough pressure because shutoffs to the water supply of Sarajevo had already started. Zetra was vanishing in flames. The manager of the Center, Enes Terzić, was there and I began to interview him. He started crying . . . I did too. The designers Djapa and Alikalfić and many others who worked on Zetra came to the scene, but nothing could be done. That night, under the red sky of Sarajevo into which the Olympiad's favorite child was vanishing, as they destroyed part of our identity but not us, we vowed that, one day, we would build an even bigger and more beautiful arena."

As he was telling this story, Nikola Bilić, the dean of Sarajevo's sports reporters, the man who interrupted a radio program for the first time in the history of Bosnia and Herzegovina in order to announce the fantastic news from Athens, couldn't hold back his tears, not even sixteen years after Athens and two years after the fire at Zetra. It is simply impossible not to cry when you manage to get within sight of the former beauty—now lying low at the bottom of the hills from which they're killing us, beneath tons of rubble from its copper roof, propped up by hundreds of new graves on the nearby soccer field. That graveyard—it seems—is also the eternal resting place of Pierre de Coubertin, the founding father of the modern Olympics, who probably spent the best days of his life in Sarajevo, but also died here.

Bosnian Spite

"Today is the six-hundred-seventy-fourth day of the siege of Sarajevo and one day after the massacre at the marketplace in the center of town. Just as many days have passed since I've been confined here to the same thousand square meters, not one step beyond that magic circle. Friends, family, business, bombs, concerts, death—everything within the same square kilometer. Yesterday, at the time of the explosion, we were only two hundred meters away, at the awards ceremony for Sarajevo's best athletes. Can you imagine, the best athletes in this city? About three hundred people came to see, to meet and greet friends. At the same time, a hundred meters from us, in the Presidency Building, the hundredth war concert of the Sarajevo String Quartet was being held. There was a large crowd there, too, about two hundred people. Half an hour later, again about a hundred meters from the bloody marketplace, there was a performance by Chamber Theater 55. When we heard the explosion, we knew it had to be terrible. Saturday about noon, the marketplace, hundreds of people in one spot. And it *was* terrible. It was horrible. I know all those professionally connected with evil and tragedy in any way whatsoever went there right away. The organizers of the award ceremony only paused for a few minutes to think whether or not to go on. And they did. The concert at the Presidency Building also went on as planned. Mozart, Beethoven, Bach . . . The play at the Chamber Theater started on time, and those who came watched in absolute silence. Nobody tried to explain to anybody why it was so and how it was possible. Here in Sarajevo, it can't be otherwise. If it were otherwise, it wouldn't be Sarajevo. I don't know what else to call the force behind it, or whether it can be translated into any other language, but I think the only real name for it is *inat*—Bosnian spite. It is on that spite that we function. I remember I once gave up my position of general manager at *Oslobodenje* because the entire leadership of Bosnia and Herzegovina had turned its back on me just because I was defending my principles from 'professional' rogues. I'm glad I acted the way I did. Back then there were only a handful of us among the leaders of former Yugoslavia who openly opposed Milošević, trying to show where his nationalism and fascism were taking us. They got rid of us because of that, but I don't care. I was happy we didn't give in. Later on I started an airline company with some friends. Everybody told us it was crazy, that it wasn't just child's play. In four months and eight days we had over seven hundred flights carrying about forty thousand passengers, mostly on international lines. We started from zero and, four months later, we had four and a half million dollars in our account. Then came the war and this place here was bombed three times. We've fixed it, we'll start again. What else can you do? I know that if you stick to your guns, you can always start again. We're ready to go again, as soon as the destruction stops. It has to stop. Maybe it would have been 'normal,' at the beginning, for me to get on a company plane and take me and my family to a safe place. But to me that *wasn't* normal. It isn't to any Sarajevan. I am not saying that I won't look after my children, I'm not saying they will suffer the third winter in a row in this place, but I know where I belong—to the bitter end. At least until a new beginning in this city, when we are again part of the 'civilized' world. If you think it's out of spite, so be it. Or maybe it's something else. All I know is there isn't any other way, at least if you still want to get up in the morning and look at yourself in the mirror.

> *Muhamed Abadžić, owner and manager of Air-Comerc*

A Letter to His Excellency

Nada Salom the journalist is a Serb on her mother's side, Slovenian on her father's, Jewish because of her last name and a Sarajevan, through and through. A heart of pure gold, she has remained my truest friend since our days at school together. After a short "exit" she came back to her city, opened the door of the editorial office at *Oslobodenje*, and said to me, barely holding herself back, "Zlatko, now I know everything, I've finally seen the light. God, how happy I am to be here again."

We've been working together at *Oslobodenje* for twenty years now, moving from one job to another, but nearly always staying together. For twenty years we've shared our high-school memories when we began as "journalists" on *Elan,* the school paper, with our first poems and drawings. She never stopped talking about an Eiffel Tower that I drew for *Elan*—she says she still has it—and I feel bad telling her that I didn't have a clue about the Eiffel Tower. Nor do I remember hundreds of little stories that she keeps repeating and that we used to tell each other in those days, in that earlier Sarajevo of ours. I only remember our trip to Egypt with friends just before this war and her obsession with the dazzling light there, with Sinai, with the monastery of St. Catherine. We vowed to come again, sooner or later. We had no idea, we the children of Sarajevo, that the war was already beginning, that someone had planned it and the trigger had already been pulled. The stupid children of Sarajevo.

Then Nada's son Robert went to England. He meant the world to her. At first, there were a few phone conversations between them, then occasional letters that traveled two or three months, and after that, total silence.

One day we got the news from Strasbourg that *Oslobodenje* had been awarded the 1993 Sakharov Prize by the European Parliament. (They obviously needed to calm their conscience about Bosnia.) It was decided that three of us from the editorial board should go to the ceremony. Then it seemed, like now, that it was quite logical for Nada to go to Strasbourg. After all, Nada had been working stubbornly for two years on subjects that we all thought, early in the war, slightly ridiculous, i.e. "cultural" topics. But, in the course of time, those things turned out to be precisely what characterized the true spirit of Sarajevo. I also knew that it would give Nada a chance to spend a few days in London with her son Robert and "recharge her batteries" for the hundreds and hundreds of days of war and suffering that were sure to follow.

I'll never know for sure why Nada's room at the Sofitel in Strasbourg stayed empty those December days when we were presented with the Sakharov Prize. Everything had been arranged for her trip, but someone somewhere, most likely in Sarajevo, had "pulled the brakes" on it. Nada was late for Strasbourg, and those distinguished Englishmen from the European Parliament, who celebrated the prize with us and who were in a position to arrange for her two-week tourist visa to Britain with a wink of an eye, had gone home for Christmas. It was all so sad. My friend was forced to flounder around Slovenia for weeks, not knowing what to do or where to go. One day the news reached Sarajevo that she had managed to "enter" the island. There was a lot of speculation about it, except for one thing: nobody doubted for a second that Nada would come back. Of this, I don't even think there was any doubt in the minds of those who prevented her from going to Strasbourg.

In early February 1994, just before the marketplace massacre, a different Nada Salom came back to Sarajevo. From there she sent a letter to Zagreb through some friends to His Excellency Mr. Brian Sparrow, the British ambassador to Croatia.

"Your Excellency,

I do not know how to begin this letter. I am not yet capable of—as we say—gathering my wits after my first stay out of Sarajevo and my return to this city. I hope that you will forgive me for writing in a confused way, both you and the three hundred people I promised to bring letters from their loved ones. All those letters began 'I have the opportunity to send you a letter with a journalist who is returning to Sarajevo. I apologize for my messy writing, it is hard to do it in haste and make it short because she is not allowed to take more than six letters, so all the letters will be without envelopes, since she will put them with her own mail . . .'"

That is what I did and I managed to bring a third of the letters in my baggage. I am waiting for the bag with my personal effects and the remaining letters to arrive through a "special connection." These days, while sorting out the letters and setting aside the ones addressed to me and my family, I am wondering if there is a way for me to send you a picture postcard of Sarajevo, as I wanted to on January 13, 1994, on my way out of the Cibona Building in Zagreb, where your embassy is located. I will always remember that morning and the joy which my colleague Lidija Krslak, a journalist from Sarajevo on a 'temporary' assignment in Zagreb, shared with me as I cried, this time from happiness, holding firmly onto my blue passport with lilies, which contained my visa: Valid for presentation at a United Kingdom port until 13 July 1994; date of issue: 13 January 1994.

That morning everything went smoothly. As soon as I appeared at the door of your embassy, a polite clerk asked for my passport and in two or three minutes gave it back to me with the visa.

Your Excellency—you will remember that you were addressed in the same way in the letter written to you by the general manager of *Oslobodenje*, the newspaper for which I have been working for over two decades, on his own behalf as well as on behalf of the paper's entire staff.

You were not in Zagreb at the time, but your clerks zealously fulfilled their duties. The fact that I was coming from Sarajevo, from Bosnia-Herzegovina, was the strongest argument against which all the papers I had as guarantees for my visit to your country were considered worthless. After two interviews, the officially stamped rejection was handed over, with the following explanation: 'You requested a visa to visit Great Britain for a period of two weeks, but I cannot be certain that you will leave Great Britain at the end of your visit. You have very little reason to go back to your city, Sarajevo, a place where the situation is difficult.'

God, I clamped down hard on my temples so my blood wouldn't start boiling, so my skull wouldn't explode. Has the whole world gone stark, raving mad? Can a clerk (I am excusing this man, whose identity I don't even know, but who—I repeat—was simply carrying out his duty), who in his 'questioning' did not once ask me what things were really like in Sarajevo, write something like that? I wanted to just scream in front of the locked doors of the embassy that thirtieth of December as people all around me rushed home with the spirit of the upcoming New Year. Does anyone in the world have the right to tell me, or anyone else from Sarajevo, something like this? Even if we seem completely abnormal, it is we who are Sarajevo. A city, as you well know, Your Excellency, is made of people, not houses. Just like London, your capital, where, or at least so I believe, there must be space for hundreds of our refugees. And they could even live a decent life.

I gladly went back to my city and I have been thinking all this time about how I could get in touch with you. I am doing it like this, taking advantage of my privileged position as a journalist. Actually, it is only like this that I exist at all, for as a citizen of this country of mine I can't go anywhere. My passport is a red rag to bulls waiting at all the entrances and exits; and as for the search for visas, asylum status, letters of guarantee and the like, many things can be written. Most of all, a lot can be written of the single question that I was asked incessantly by my compatriots while I was away: When and how will you get back?

You managed to see a picture-postcard view of Sarajevo through the lens of a TV camera on the February 5, 1994, the first day after I returned to my city. You could see that area around the cathedral particularly well, where the marketplace is. And this time too, I was lucky. I didn't get to the market, but got held up visiting a friend. Later on in the day, using the last shreds of strength I had left, trembling like a leaf, I forced myself to look at the reports on TV for, as the poet Avdo Sidran says, 'they are all my people.' I knew and recognized all of them as the Pale-Belgrade broadcast explained that this was a case of old corpses and the body parts of plastic dummies. While my heart savagely beat against my throat, I, who have never had much under-standing of any kind of armaments except for stage props, listened in despair as military 'experts' pointed out that the weapons in question here were 'antipedestrian, ministatic or ricochet-activated circularly cutting units that we just bring in and place before going and hiding behind another pedestrian. A graduated chart of artillery hits, under ideal conditions, shows that of 1,800 fragments prior to detonation, only 400 kill animals on the firing range . . .' With craters in my stomach, I listened to the explanations and continued writing this letter since I'm sure you know I am made of flesh and blood, that I'm not a doll, that I have been in your country and that I've come back to my city, 'Sarajevo, where the situation is extremely dif-ficult.'

I would like to thank you again for the trust you placed in me by granting me a visa to visit your country. In the hope that you will once come to visit my city and that I will be able to show you what we consider cultural and spiritual resistance, let me read you some lines by Ivo Andrić: 'It was just God turning His face momentarily and leaving the world in darkness, while you howl: "victory," when there is no victory but only a meagre, bloody lie and one great big calamity.'

Wishing you all the best.

Sincerely yours,

Nada Salom"

That is the letter addressed to His Excellency, the British ambassador in Zagreb. How fond I am of my friend Nada! We'll go on trips again, and visit other newspapers with our Sarajevan friends. The only thing I'm not sure of is whether or not we'll visit those terribly important and terribly serious, civilized countries to whose ambassadors you have to write long letters before they let you in for a short time so you can see your next of kin or get to know a small part of their terribly important civilization. Civilization also exists, I daresay, in places where you don't need a visa to get in.

Like Sarajevo, for instance.

Shrapnel

". . . Grandma, can't you see it's falling all over the place? Why do you have to walk through the middle of the street? Get in a shelter till it passes, you'll get killed by a piece of shrapnel."

"That's exactly why I'm walking in the middle of the street, to get killed. But I won't, my son, unfortunately I won't. I've been trying for months . . ."

Tito Street, January 2, 1994

An Ordinary Miracle

Throughout this grim time of war, the world keeps closing every door and window through which any ray of optimism and hope can shine, even for a second, to brighten up this forlorn warscape. If any hope was left after the second year of solitude, it was thanks to people who thought nothing of what the world considered a miracle; people who, with extraordinary enthusiasm, considered entirely ordinary what was thought of as impossible out there in the world. Taib Šahinpašić, owner of a bookstore in Sarajevo, presented his devastated city with such a "mundane miracle" on a March morning in 1993 when he opened an exhibit of foreign books in the former Literary Museum, near the treacherous and totally deserted promenades along the Miljacka. By its rich array, the number of titles, variety and quality of books, the exhibit could have stood its own in those "sophisticated" places out there, in more normal times. Taib Šahinpašić not only opened an exhibit, but a door to optimism; by restoring belief in the future he challenged the vandals who in the name of brute force had already burned every book within their reach. He brought Sarajevo back into the cycle of information and knowledge that revolves around civilization's beaten paths.

"In those days I hovered in the air more than walked the earth. At the opening, there were a few hundred people, and the shooting was heavy. People stopped at the entrance to the museum, and everyone looked kind of surprised but soon they were smiling. Students, professors, academics, couples, or just ordinary kids would come day after day and stay for hours leafing through the wonders from 'that' world which I happened to have at the beginning of the war. Some books were actually published in the first year of the war—1992. I was extremely proud of myself, of Sarajevo and all our people. Then a foreign journalist asked me how such a thing was possible, and whether or not I considered the whole thing a miracle. I said it was nothing of the kind because if books were a miracle in Sarajevo I wouldn't have had five thousand foreign books in my private book-store before the war. In fact, it's exactly the opposite, but people out there refuse to recognize this. *Not* having access to such books in Sarajevo is the strange thing, not this.

"Then, I had a real brainstorm. I decided that we should organize a big international book fair every other year. All those people that have been 'devouring' books during this war deserve it. And I'm quite serious about this. Even if I don't find anyone else to help me, I'll do it myself, no matter what it costs."

This ordinary man, Taib, dealing with even more ordinary Sara-jevans, brings, sends, buys, sells, and gives away most of the books he has in stock every day, saving only a few for better times and his ever-present dream of a "big international book fair in Sarajevo." As if what he did in March '93 wasn't big enough. One thing is sure, though: he won't have to organize that fair by himself, as he said. Every now and then, who knows exactly how, letters come to our ruined city from publishers who realize precisely what kind of place and what kind of people are at stake in this battle. The offers are honest and serious. Sarajevo will, no doubt, have its own book fair. The only problem is, as Taib Šahinpašić says, that the first few will have to stay up for a long time "until people catch up and read all the foreign books they missed. After that everything will go a lot more smoothly. . . ."

Kidnapping Clinton

On January 28, 1994, late at night, the local radio station Zid [Wall] announced "the news of the day": a guy from Sarajevo by the name of Džemo, now living somewhere in the States, finally managed, after a few failed attempts, to kidnap Bill Clinton. The report said that Džemo disappeared to whereabouts unknown with Clinton and that, several hours after this unprecedented operation, he called an American TV station to say he would take Clinton to Sarajevo and show him what is happening here, or else he would gouge his eyes out and bring them to Sarajevo so the president could see the situation "with his own eyes."

The news is, of course, an integral part of Radio Zid's editorial policy, since they found themselves mirroring the very situation of every urbane Sarajevan: every drama, even our own, turns grotesque at some point and ends up becoming part of the general insanity that has gripped the city's spirit these two years.

After this news item hundreds of Zid listeners joined in spontaneously, embellishing the uproar that had already been provoked with their own share of imagination. Spiteful resistance to the "Clintonization" and "Mitterandization" of the world across the radio waves turned into a wild spree that everybody wanted to join in their own way. People who confirmed they knew Džemo called in, saying that he "most certainly went to Washington to kidnap the president, because that's just like him." Others said they were "Džemo's neighbors, and it's true that he's prepared to gouge someone's eyes out for Sarajevo . . ." A school friend of Džemo's insisted that the news was "a hundred percent true, because I know my friend, he is a great guy and, yes, he did always say, when he was mad, that he would gouge someone's eyes out."

The story went on through the night and even began to appear real, in spite of the fact that everyone knew from the very beginning that Radio Zid was only fabricating gallows humor out of suffering, darkness, and madness, the kind of entertainment half of Sarajevo was only too eager to be a part of.

I have a neighbor by the name of Nino, a driver in the once large Sarajevan company Hidrogradnja. He became an invalid at the beginning of the war after the infamous incident at the bakery on Vaso Miskin Street. Now he's opened a workshop in his garage, where he tends to all the mechanical problems of the tenants in his building. He understood the story of the Clinton kidnapping somewhat differently. Actually, Nino *would* have understood the story the way everyone else did, but he and his wife Mina had overslept so they missed the beginning. At some point Nino and Mina found themselves getting caught up in the Zid story; at first they only chuckled a bit, and then, looking at each other in the candlelit room, they almost unconsciously began silencing each other so they could listen carefully to every word that was coming over the air. And there was a lot to hear, too. First, "local politicians" called in to warn that "the gentleman's action might be counterproductive for our young democratic country," then Suljo from the "front lines" called in and told one of the politicians "not to bullshit too much but grab a gun and come to the front lines, and as far as Džemo was concerned, he was super and the guys in the trenches thought he was aces." The discussion became quite heated as a reporter kept trying to reach America by satellite and get in on any program, since "all hell must have broken loose over there." One listener suggested launching a fund-raising campaign for cigarettes and "humanitarian aid for Džemo when he goes to jail, because America is really powerful and our poor friend will be caught sooner or later."

Sometime around midnight Nino and his wife Mina started to tune in to other stations, particularly official Radio Sarajevo, to find out what they were saying about the "news of the day." Madness, imagination, fiction and reality all intertwined in just one night and one place, in a whirl of dozens of phone calls and tales in which everyone knew everything, but it all seemed so likely.

The official radio didn't report anything. Not a word. "My God, Mina," Nino said as if to himself, "How is all this possible? Who is crazy here?"

"Forget that now, no one's crazy, just get ready and go to Vratnik [a suburb of Sarajevo] and bring our daughter here. Can't you see what this means? Americans may bomb Sarajevo even tonight. Better bring our daughter from grandma's. Let's at least have the child with us . . ."

Nino didn't go across town that night to get his daughter from grandma's. Partly because of the curfew. "It would be counterproductive," he said to his wife, "if they catch me out on the street. They'll put me in jail so I won't even be home when the chaos starts." Maybe he also suspected, in the very back of his mind, that something wasn't quite on the level. Not that Americans wouldn't bomb Sarajevo but "how could Džemo gouge out a man's eyes just like that. Not just like that. That's not done in Sarajevo. A guy that has the balls to kidnap Clinton is not the kind of guy that would commit such an atrocity." There, that was the weak point of the story, at least according to Nino's logic. "That doesn't seem like something a guy from Sarajevo would do," he said the next morning, talking about his sleepless night and puffing away at a pipe that hadn't had a speck of tobacco in it for years. "And yet, you know, everything somehow seemed possible. And why wouldn't it be possible when you see what they're doing to us. Two years ago I would have thought I was crazy if I turned on the radio in the middle of the night and heard that someone would bomb Sarajevo and do everything they are doing to us now, and even get away with it. Now anything is possible. No one is crazy, and everyone is crazy. . . ."

The following night a local station transmitted an item stating that, in a few days, the gas pipes would open again in Sarajevo, there would be more electricity, and water pressure was going to get better. No one called anyone else by phone, except for a sleepy voice calling the station to say: "Don't talk nonsense, we're not idiots. Give us music, so we can get some sleep."

The Man Who Likes Pelé

Those hot days in the summer of 1992, when no one in Sarajevo fully grasped what hit them, when death lay in wait at every street corner because the city itself had not been cleansed of snipers, the most dangerous route in Sarajevo was, without a doubt, the one going along Marshal Tito Barracks. On either side of that building, every meter was "covered" by snipers' sights. By killing the civilians, they "defended Serbia and Yugoslavia."

People who, in spite of everything, had to venture through there to get to the other side of the city, said that passing the barracks was equivalent to a "premeditated suicide" Others simply called the passage a game of Russian roulette. It is hard to tell nowadays who was closer to the truth. Nevertheless, no one among those who regularly challenged destiny by passing the barracks disagreed about one thing: the most stubborn challenger, the calmest, and the most regular was Tomislav Počanić. Known as Tomo among his friends, he was one of Sarajevo's great sports reporters, always smiling, always with a pile of newspapers under his arm, a walking encyclopedia on tennis, boxing, football, handball . . . His kindness is immeasurable, and in the editorial offices of *Oslobodenje*, he serves as a "maid-of-all-work."

Steadily and without a single day of rest, Tomo challenged an already aggravated destiny. He passed the dangerous route on his way to the newspaper building or, on the side of the barracks, on the way home. He walked more or less quickly, sometimes stopping for a moment behind a wall or some other barrier, just long enough to scan the road in front of him. Terrifying all his friends, he walked by the railroad station, on the side nearest the barracks windows, hidden by sandbags with snipers lurking behind them. "If they decide to do it, that's it," Tomo would say. Having made it to the *Oslobodenje* building, he would appear surprised by our looks and questions. We cracked jokes about "tips Tomo was getting from the barracks." Others figured the snipers realized they were dealing with a nice guy, totally detached from this world, too busy with goals, baskets, knockouts, statistics, and glorious moments in sports that he didn't even have time to find his bearings.

"How out of this world everything seemed that Olympic winter in 1984! You know, that's more or less how I've always imagined paradise: a blissful atmosphere, smiles, beauty, kindness and sweetness all around. Everything bathed in light, in the white of the snow, in music. And all that thanks to sports. Imagine . . . Someone accidentally bumps into you on the street and apologizes immediately, asks if you need any help. You want to pay for your taxi and the driver says, 'Forget it. That's for the Olympiad, for sports.' Those wretches who now say that we can't live together, what do they know? I remember that genius, that soccer legend, the beloved Edson Arantes de Nascimento Pelé I remember how what he said made us love him even more: 'I'd like to be remembered as everybody's friend. But my main reason for being proud of myself is that nobody will be able to say that I supported only one religion, only one nation, only one skin color. As far as I'm concerned, there is no difference among people.' Those were his very words.

Even now, with a pile of newspapers tucked under his arm, in his old raincoat, slightly stooped but with a quick step, Tomo passes the barracks twice a day, though they are no longer barracks. Abandoned in the fall of 1992, they were set on fire and forgotten. Routinely walking around town like Tomislav Počanić, Tomo still falls within the domain of "premeditated suicide" or, at the very least, Russian roulette; for everybody, that is, except him, since he is simply carrying on with his life and work.

And it seems to me quite natural that Tomo should adore Pelé. Pelé too, would have liked him if he had met him, of that I am absolutely sure.

Camus Would Turn Over in His Grave

Mediha Filipović, a professor at the School of Dentistry, was known in Sarajevo as the "French lady." Always smiling, always elegant, she looked like a person who never had a complex over anything. She traveled when few traveled, recited French poetry, sang French songs. She liked to say how she "first learned French, then our language." So it just seemed natural to us that Meda, as we called her, went to France for her specialization, to Nantes, with Professor Jean Delaire. Even then she would say with a smile, "They go there from all over France to specialize, so why shouldn't I?" She wrote beautiful letters from Nantes and Paris, making us jealous that she had become part of a world we only dreamed of. She wrote about impressionists and classics, about palaces on the Loire and existentialists, about the Louvre and Versailles. She wrote of how much she loved all such things. That was when no one knew about politics or what would come.

She stayed in Sarajevo throughout the war. Some people deceived her in early 1992 by sending her papers for a job in Qatar, in the United Arab Emirates, then never getting in touch with her again. "Those are our Muslim brothers," she said with a bitter smile when we met in one of Sarajevo's "reawakened" cafés. Still, she spoke with much more bitterness and anger about her "French people." That bitterness, as she said, came from the feeling that "your own people" betrayed you.

"I don't care about Qatar. Being tricked by those guys is like being tricked by someone I never knew, so I couldn't really expect anything from them. But France was my whole life! I invested all my emotions, all my education, thousands of sleepless nights in their culture, their history and tradition. And what of it today? I was in Paris that May 8, 1981, when the Socialists and Mitterand came to power. I celebrated like crazy with thousands of others. We celebrated democracy, we celebrated the future. We were complete idiots because we knew nothing about politics, about 'big interests,' about lies and deceipts. My first real shock came from the story about Bokassa, his crowning and everything that went with it. And then, all the events that followed. All those efforts to protect, at any cost, the biggest fascists and the biggest criminals on the face of the earth. All that diplomacy that refused to recognize a Bogdan Bogdanović, a Mirko Kovač, or a Živorad Kovačević among the Serbs, but recognized Slobodan Milošević, Šešelj, Arkan and the like. How was such a choice made, on the basis of French culture, French classics, the French revolution?

"It's not only Bosnia and Sarajevo they have betrayed. More than us, they've betrayed themselves and their own history. Because of France, I went to a classical gymnasium. In the professional sense I 'grew up' with the ODF review, and today, after all this, I'm not sure that I ever want to see Paris and France again. They've made the choice for me, not me or my friends. They chose Karadžić, and not someone who was their student, in the true sense of the word. Albert Camus would turn over in his grave if he could see what they chose. His *Plague* is a joke compared to our plague, a plague they helped bring about, the same people who defended Bokassa, Milošević and so many others. There, now I can have a good cry."

A Letter to the World's Musicians

Lejla Jusić is a girl who makes Sarajevo's nights and days different—you could almost say beautiful—with songs accompanied by guitar and piano. Those who don't know her and hear her for the first time can hardly resist asking: where was she before, where did she come from, how come we didn't know about her? Some of those who came to Sarajevo from abroad and heard Lejla sing could hardly believe it. "And did you learn to sing and play so well during the war?" a German journalist asked Lejla after a "Sarajevan Night" held at the Jež [hedgehog] restaurant, in the center of town.

Lejla, of course, didn't learn how to sing and play during the war. She learned many other things in the war, out of misery and necessity. Out of love, she taught others to play and sing. And this prompted her to write a letter to the musicians of the world. On January 31, 1994, she "explained" what it was like to be a musician in Sarajevo:

"July 1992.

In a makeshift shelter, where they've already lived two months since it's impossible to survive in the apartment, I watch two girls as they rush to use the electricity that came on by chance to record songs, so they can copy the lyrics in their diaries later. The song that seems to interest them the most is Kemal Monteno's 'Sarajevo, My Love,' because they've begun to understand the lyrics. So the song becomes a part of them, like everyone who loves this city. I remember that even as a little girl, I always sang that song when we came back from the Adriatic coast. I still mumbled the text and changed the words around, but those three words, *Sarajevo, my love,* I pronounced flawlessly. Later on, too, whenever I would come back from tours and trips around the world, the melody of that song always came back to me.

Because the texts were neatly copied, little Gina—a thirteen-year-old girl who had been learning to play the accordion in school before the war—came to me with a guitar and begged me to write the chords for her. She decided to learn how to play the guitar as well, since she had plenty of time on her hands. Playing outside could be fatal since the first front line is two hundred meters down the street and the second only one streetcar stop further. She'd been out of school for three months already, so she hadn't seen her friends from class for a long time either. Like all of us, though, she made new friends among her neighbors, but still spent most of her time with me because there was a stronger bond between us, something that, in all this evil around us, still has a righteous place— music. And, indeed, you could hear songs coming out of that shelter, marked by the rhythm of the detonating shells.

This January, in the year 1994 of the war, Gina is already a young lady, fifteen years old, no longer a kid. She's learned how to play the guitar, says she isn't afraid of the grenades anymore but, unfortunately, many of her friends got killed. All kinds of memories bind us to that shelter. It reminds me of the first days of the war, when we didn't know what to expect, when we experienced every shell differently. It also reminds me of the music we made and the time we spent together. The song 'Sarajevo, My Love' remained the anthem of the shelter.

The spirit of Sarajevo, dear colleagues, has triumphed again. That's why I want to tell you something. We don't need orchestras because we can still play the old instruments, safely hidden away. We don't need new music because we have the inspiration to create. But, please, at least try to set the pitch for life beyond and a new kind of music, or do we have to do it for you?"

Many learned how to sing and play in the war, like fifteen-year-old Gina. Those children will surely sing after the war as well. Why else would they learn in basements and cellars? Those who knew how to sing and play before the war won't forget. Songs in Sarajevo can't be forgotten, only taught and learned again and again.

Yellow Quinces

If you don't know Davorin Popović, aka Pimpek, Dačo, the Singer, and Genius, you don't know anything about Sarajevo, its young people, about Fis or Young Bosnia, the Sloga dance hall that five days of the week you prepare for so you can tremble with excitement the sixth and seventh days listening to the voice of Davorin and the group Indexi, so you can shudder when the lights are dimmed for "ladies' choice" and slow dancing.

You don't know anything about Sarajevo if you don't remember the day when the most celebrated Yugoslav basketball team played Sarajevo in an exhibition match at the Fis. It was then that the Yugoslavs demanded our coach take Pimpek-Dačo-Genius out of the game because "if anybody's going to look like fools it won't be us but you." Not knowing this also means you don't know the story of Davorin-Dačo the genius, arm in arm with two TV cameramen, setting out to Bulozi, on the way to Pale. The "Serb heroes" had entrenched themselves up there already, but he tried to talk them into going back to where they came from. They listened to him "because those cretins thought I was a Serb since my last name is Popović."

Luckily, though, there aren't many people left in town who know nothing about it, i.e. about Davorin, Dačo, Pimpek, and the Singer, as he is affectionately called by his best friend Kemal Monteno.

Sarajevo's living legends, of whom Dačo was always one, became what they are today when they lost their mythical aura to become ordinary, simple, everyday Sarajevans. Without them, this city would not be what it is, without them Sarajevo could not exist. "The guys

117

here respected me a lot more when Dačo asked me to buy him some cigarettes. Other kids foamed at the mouth seeing that God had trust in me," said another Kemo early on in the war; he's gone on to become the commander of a special unit on a sensitive section of the city defense lines. "You know, Zlaja, he played it just right. He knew it would make me look good with the girls, but he made out as if he didn't see it. . . . When I found out, at the time, that he'd gone to Bulozi, I thought it was amazing. You know what he did with them up there? He offered them two hundred thousand marks if they would leave, and he nearly tricked them."

"Why nearly?" Davorin intervened. "They'd accepted the offer, but I had a small problem: I didn't have two hundred thousand marks to complete the operation. Tough luck . . ."

With Davorin Popović in Sarajevo, we should really mention those no longer in the city, although they are inseparable from the stories that typify Sarajevo. According to Davorin, there is a strange resemblance between their situation and the song "Yellow Quinces." That song is another item of Sarajevo's culture without which this city could not exist. Let them wonder why.

> *Two young people were in love*
> *for six months and a year*
> *when they wanted to join in marriage*
> *their enemies wouldn't let them be . . .*
> *Beautiful Fatma wasted away*
> *her mother's only daughter*
> *she longed for yellow quinces*
> *yellow quinces from Istanbul . . .*
> *He went to find them, her beloved,*
> *to find yellow quinces in Istanbul,*
> *but didn't come back for three years*
> *he never arrived nor even sent a missive*
> *When he brought the quinces,*
> *when he arrived, his beloved*
> *Fatma lay resting in her coffin.*

I'll give two hundred pieces if you let her go
I'll give three hundred if you unveil her
so I can kiss my Fatma just once more . . .

"I don't hold it against them. I don't hold it against anybody. Kemo and I got a letter recently, from Italy. It said: 'Here we are in a nice little restaurant, drinking fresh *vino rosso*, eating, and thinking about you—we know it's tough for you there.' OK, very nice, if you want to be nasty. I'm happy they're drinking *vino rosso* while we're dying, but that wine has nothing to do with us anymore. They're not ours anymore, they're no longer *from* here, they don't have the feeling of belonging 'here' because this isn't their world, they have no bond left to this place. As for me, I belong 'here,' I would never go off 'to Istanbul' for three years and let my people die waiting for me. *This* is where my yellow quinces are. If I did go someplace to look for them, it wouldn't be for long. Muhamed Kreševljaković, the mayor, asked me the other day why I thought the city belonged to me. It's very simple, I said to him, it's mine, I was born here, all my folks were born here, it's me. Where could I go? And why? It doesn't bother me that some people can leave and do leave. What's painful is when they don't remember, when they forget. You see, it's like in '*Yellow Quinces*': in the end he wants to kiss her, to see her. They'll want to do the same thing one day, but it'll be too late, my dear friend, too late! Where were they during the shooting, when we suffered? After that it's too late, I'm telling you. That's why it's beautiful when someone doesn't forget you. Our friend Halid, for instance, remembered us. He gave some money to a guy who was coming back here, and he told him, 'Here, buy Kemo and Dačo a drink or two.' I don't know how much he gave, but the main thing is that he thought of it. Another buddy remembered us, with half a pint of brandy. I am grateful to him. Kemo and I need a couple of pints of brandy and a couple of pints of memories. No more than that. The bottom line is that life is summed up in just that, in a few yellow quinces. It's the thread you either hold onto or don't. There's nothing in between."

Resisting Madness

"We're all crazy, by now, in one way or another. The story is over, we've reached the point of no return. The worst thing is that we don't even know what will come to the surface when all of this stops one day. Only people who still have enough strength to suppress everything around them look normal now, all those things that, in any normal situation, would be enough to trigger a mental disorder."

These words were spoken in early 1994 by Dr. Ismet Cerić, the head of the psychiatric clinic at Sarajevo University Hospital. He is one of the most respected doctors in Sarajevo, someone who refused to leave the city although he probably could have. He used to be a "colleague" of Radovan Karadžić, the leader of those Serbs in Bosnia and Herzegovina who claim that living together with people of a different origin, a different nationality and having different names has never been nor ever will be possible. These are the pillars upon which Karadžić led his followers to carry out a genocide.

Speaking calmly about his former colleague, even a little surprised at the mention of his name, Dr. Cerić said: "Many foreign journalists who come to the Clinic to talk to us wrap up their visit with a question about Karadžić. And every time they seem to want to get us to label him as crazy, as abnormal; they usually even offer some amateur diagnosis to prove their point. We never thought he was crazy, nor do we think so now. In fact, for months now no one has had *anything* at all to say about him. As if he never even existed. If no one has anything to say about a person who worked here for close to twenty years, that already says it all. To us, he simply no longer exists. What exists are the struggles of people we can never forget, no matter how few know of their plight. Here, look at this letter by a young woman from outside Sarajevo, written after everything that happened to her at the beginning of the war. She came to see us twice, we talked for a long time, and then she disappeared. I haven't seen her since.

Here is part of that letter:

". . . One day in late July 1992, a little after 10 P.M., a car with all its parking lights on stopped in front of our house. The house was surrounded, three men kicked the door open, caught me, and put the barrels of their machine guns on my mother's stomach. One of them wanted to kill her, and another one seemed to be against it. They put a stocking over my head and carried me into the car. They pushed me to the floor, under their feet. I didn't know where they were taking me. After a short ride they took me out and up some stairs. I stumbled because I still had the stocking on my head. When they told me to stop walking, a *chetnik* grabbed my stocking and hair together and started bumping my head against the wall. I felt warm blood running down my head and getting the stocking wet. They took me into a room and ordered me to take off the stocking. I saw that I was in a hotel room and that there was a huge *chetnik* in front of me. He asked my name, how much property we had, and why our house was big. 'Turks have no right to live, let alone own property,' he said. He cursed my 'Turkish' mother and beat me. He kept hitting me on the head with his handgun. Then he put a bullet in the barrel, ready to kill me. I kept quiet and waited to die as I watched the face of a man wrenched by hatred. I didn't cry because the last drop of blood in me was frozen. I just kept quiet and clenched my teeth to stop myself from screaming. I was so badly beaten that I couldn't even stand on my feet. He ordered me to take off my clothes. I did so. He hit my chest with his fists. He ordered me to lie down. I did so. He spread my legs and pushed his hand in, saying, 'You, Turkish whore, let's see if you hid any gold in here.' The pain pulsed through my head as I looked on mutely, unable to do anything. He took off his pants and my eye caught the belt with his handgun on it. Could I grab it and kill him and myself? In the mirror opposite the bed I saw a guard watching everything. After he did that thing, he put his clothes back on. When he saw that he too was covered with blood, he slapped me twice and I saw all the stars in heaven. He went away saying that a hundred and twenty captured women were going to be killed that night. Then others came in one by one. I tried to stay conscious. I counted five of them before I fainted. Then someone slapped me on the face and I came to, but lost consciousness again soon. That, at least, is what seems to have happened. I was brought back to by a *chetnik* who said he was also supposed to take me but that I disgusted him. I managed to say that they made me disgusted at all men, from those not yet born to the hundred-year-olds. When he saw how bloody I was, he brought two pitchers of water and gave me a wash. Then he went to get more water, telling me not to open the door unless I heard his voice. He came back quickly with two more pitchers of water, and I tried to wash on my own. I didn't really care so much about washing, I wanted to see my mother. The *chetnik* said to walk, but I couldn't, so he practically carried me. There were a lot of steps going down. He put me in the car, half dead. I thought he would throw me into the Bosna River. But he didn't. He took me back home. I was met at the door by my mother, who was shocked by what they had done to me. She started screaming and cursing the *chetnik,* and he left. It was almost 4 A.M. Mom brought a potful of ice-cold water from our well and gave me a bath. I didn't cry, I just kept looking at nothing. Later Mom told me that, as soon as I was taken away, she went to T. Vasilija and, with her, to Mitar Mamaga. Mitar took Mom to the *chetniks'* headquarters and police station, where my mom insisted that she be killed too. Branka Maksimović slapped Mitar Mamaga and, with her gun, threatened to kill him for bringing a Turkish woman to headquarters. Mom says that someone from the police station immediately went to look for me and bring me home. The next day I broke everything in the house that was there to be broken. They brought me a doctor, who gave me a shot. I was all bruises and wounds. I urinated pure blood. After about three weeks I told a neighbor that I was pregnant. I thought they wouldn't kill me if I was pregnant, and I was right. Later on, when we said we wanted to leave the area, they asked for a thousand marks per person, three thousand for the three of us. I didn't have the money and nobody dared take me out. My hands kept shaking. The driver, G.R., who had brought me home that night, offered to take me out as far as Kiseljak. I didn't trust him. I was even afraid of a small boy. He told me there were fifteen of them that night and the leader's name was Gaga from Vogošća.

UNICEF organized a week of peace. There was a new head of the local police. Živko Lazarević replaced Maksimović, who refused to let us go. Our neighbors took everything from our house. The cow, the calf, the sheep, the lambs, the hens, the dog, the hay, two cars, the lawn mower, the trailer, even Mom's galoshes. Everything was taken by B. Janja and others. They let us out November 11. I go for therapy to Dr. Šada Hadžišehović, who is getting on my nerves. She tells me to take a bath and forget about it, to get married and have babies, to find a job . . . My dear doctor, how can I take an eraser and erase all those horrors from my mind? How would you feel if, God forbid, it happened to you?

I am aware of the fact that nobody understands me except my mother, who went through hell just like me. I dare not go out into the street. There are men in the street who are cruel and evil."

Doctor Cerić spoke again: "There, that's what the war looks like here. It is pure nonsense to throw around estimates about the number of raped women in this dirty war, the way they do here and all around the world. I am not saying that what they write is impossible. I just want to say that nobody can tell exactly how many cases there have been. Here in Sarajevo, we have established a group to struggle against violence. We didn't even want to say that it was directly concerned with raped women, to avoid offending them. We recruited only female doctors, thinking that the women would find it easier to talk to them. You know what happened? In the course of over a year of searches and investigations, only eighteen women reported in to us. And none wanted to speak to a female doctor. I don't know why. But I know that not one of them wanted to give her name, or to say how she felt about the child that was on the way. They came to us, male doctors, and although eighteen is not a big sample, it was clear that all the young women responded in the same way: they asked for a gun so they could go find a rapist and kill him. Older women were calmer and more rational. But one thing is common to all of them: none brought the child into the story. The unborn were kept aside. Some accept the children, others don't. Actually, we usually found out about raped women after they gave birth and said they didn't want the child. Besides the girl who wrote that letter and came here twice, there was another young woman who came to try and talk through her troubles. She said what she now finds worst of all is the neighborhood ladies coming to have coffee with her, as if out of pity, and then asking her for the hundredth time to tell them how it all happened, how many men there were, how they did it, what she felt, etc. She also disappeared one day. To think that a commission of any kind, domestic or foreign, will ever determine exactly what and to what extent things happened, can only be wishful thinking.

"One of the only indications of the state of things here now is the suicide rate. Sarajevo used to be a city of very few suicides, either attempted or committed. The sad thing about the current suicides is that the people involved are usually older, leading intellectuals, university professors, prominent actors, journalists. And none of them commits suicide in any special way. It is enough to be condemned to the loneliness of a cold apartment, to dependence on humanitarian aid, and bring yourself to a state in which nobody can help you any more. I've heard people in Sarajevo talk of dying of abandonment. Horrible but true. When some of them end up in the hospital and you talk to them, you see there is nothing of life left in them. You also see that the end is coming as they persist in trying not to give themselves up to evil and aggressiveness. Those people don't see, and don't want to see, a single reason, a single element that might justify the acceptance of the crime they have been pushed into.

"In that sense, we're all in the same boat. We're all at the end of our rope, losing our nerve, done in, to use some common expressions. But we resist that push into violence, into aggression, at every step. The only question is how much longer anyone can take it. Let me repeat that, potentially, we're all insane. Only we resist madness as, I think, few have ever managed before."

Basket

Nobody knows any more whether the seige of Sarajevo will ever end. And, if and when it does, whether Sarajevo will still exist. No one, therefore, still doubts that Sarajevo can also cease to exist. What will never die, though, is the legend of Zuć Hill, the first battleground near the city where Sarajevans were "above," while they were "below." Once woods and meadows, gently sloping hills between the city and neighboring Vogošća, now it's a wasteland that looks like the desolate face of some other planet. Thousands and thousands of craters from bombs and shells testify that Zuć is not beyond the bounds of this evil and suffering. One day, stories will be told of the hill that saved Sarajevo for months from those who kept trying to take it and enter the city. But some stories that tell more about the people of Zuć than all the thousands of shells that fell there may be forgotten. One such story was told by Salko Huntić, a junior in college, as he nursed a beer in a café in the middle of town and counted the hours till the end of his three-day break before going back to his position in a trench on Zuć:

"If I survive, I don't know if I'll remember the worst single day. I don't know if it can even be remembered. And what is there to remember? I think of those days, at the beginning of the year, when about twenty thousand grenades fell on us in three days. And I know that we laughed like lunatics underground, in 'wolf lairs,' guessing how far they had fallen from us, and when it would stop so their infantry would attack. There, I remember the laughter. And something else. It was early winter. There was some fog around. My friend and I were on guard duty when, suddenly, a ten- or twelve-year-old kid showed up. We couldn't talk loud or shout because the guys on the other side were only about fifty meters away in their trenches. The kid was scared and couldn't even talk when he saw us. He tried to go back, but he couldn't. It seemed to me that he didn't even know where to go. He was carrying a little basket, covered with a clean white cloth.

'Where are you going, kid? Who are you looking for?'

"I'm going to my dad. Mother sent me to bring him lunch and another pair of socks for tonight, she says he'll be cold,' the boy managed to say.

'Where is your father? Do you know the exact place?'

'I don't. I thought he was here somewhere. I went the way Mom told me to go, but maybe I got lost.'

'What's your father's name?'

'Jovo.'

'You should know that your father Jovo is not here, he's over there for sure, on the other side.'

"The boy began to cry, gripping the basket with his cold hands. he repeated quietly that his mother would give him a beating when she learned about this. Then I stood up a little in my trench and yelled through the fog to the other side, 'Jovo, your son is here. Can you hear me?'

"Dead silence, almost a minute went by, then a voice: 'I don't believe it, you're lying to get me out of the trench.'

'We don't want to get anyone out of the trench, we just want to tell you not to shoot at the boy, he's going to walk across now to bring you lunch.'

"I told the boy not to be afraid, to run over to the other side to his father, and to get back here on the way home, since he knew the way from there and wouldn't get lost. I saw from his look that he didn't believe us. Still, he got out of the trench and started running to the other side. At one point, the white cloth fell off his basket. After a few steps he stopped, trying to figure out what to do. He darted back to pick up the cloth, dirty from the mud it had fallen into, then continued running toward the place where he heard his father's voice.

"A long time after that, for an hour or two maybe, we didn't hear anything. There was total silence. They didn't shoot, and neither did we. We all somehow thought about the boy over there in the trench. Then, suddenly, we heard Jovo's voice, now familiar, through the thickening fog: 'Hey, my boy would like to go back that way. Could you not shoot? He's going home!'

'All right,' we cried out from our end of the line.

"In a strange way I was glad I was going to see the boy again, now probably less frightened.

"He appeared suddenly out of the fog, and came sliding into our trench. The basket in his hand was full again. This time, there was a bottle corked with a piece of folded newspaper, a few apples, and a piece of homemade cheese. We thought the kid was carrying that home.

'Here, my father sent this to you. He said to drink up and have a bite. And he begs you for two cigarettes, if you have any. He hasn't seen a cigarette in three days.'

"Maybe this is a bit too much, I thought for a moment. The boy looked at us as if wanting to say something else, but seemed to hesitate. 'Com'on, kid, tell us what else your father told you?'

'He told me that they were leaving here tomorrow, and that I should tell you that they won't be shooting tonight, so if you want, both them and you can get some sleep tonight. And that tomorrow some other soldiers are taking their place, and that they will shoot a lot. They're not from here . . .'

"We tied a pack of cigarettes to a big stone. Then I got up a from the trench and shouted through the fog again, 'Jovo, catch this, and the thing for tonight is OK with us, if we can trust you.'

'We'll leave one guard and you can do the same if you want, and let's see who's straight,' he yelled from over there. 'And thanks for the kid and the cigarettes.'

"That night they didn't shoot. Neither did we. The following day, around noon, all hell broke loose. They turned the earth and the sky upside down. I never saw the boy again, or heard from Jovo. But I'll remember this story for the rest of my life."

Father

After all this I have only one wish: that my sons Ognjen and Dražen, Sarajevans and Europeans by luck or sheer circumstance, turn out like their grandfather. My father. A man killed by "natural" causes on January 9, 1994, after he himself decided it should be that way. I don't know if my sons will achieve that, since it so difficult. But even if they try, it will mean a lot to us, though mainly to them.

The night before he was laid to rest in the Lion Cemetery, where all honorable Sarajevans are buried, my father lay dead in his apartment, a place he didn't want to leave even when he could. Under a huge, somewhat naive painting of the Old Bridge at Mostar, over the unrealistically blue river Neretva. All his life he carried that painting within him. Finally, he painted it. As a painter he was an amateur but his love for that city and river was most professional, so he painted seriously and with great care.

That night his bed was surrounded by neighbors that no one in the family really knew. They came when they heard of his death, only asking if they could sit around him. "That's the least we can do for a man like that. We don't know how to tell you how much he meant to us, how nicely he spoke with us . . ." I remembered that my father had asked me for cigarettes during the past months, even though he didn't smoke. "For my friends from the block," he would say. "You know, Zlatko, they don't have any." It was then that I saw his friends from the block for the first time, at his bed on his last day in the house, under the painting of the Old Bridge. It was honorable to have the kind of friends Mustafa Dizdarević had: a high-ranking officer of an army that was finished a long time ago, a carpenter, a trolley conductor, and a retired cook.

The day before he went to bed for the last time, my father told me why he had decided not to get up again. I didn't understand it that way at the time, just as I haven't understood any of the most important things about this war. He saw me to the door and hugged me. We never hugged after visits to my parents. We had something of a "macho" relationship; as a child he taught me that men didn't display such things but that it was their duty to carry a lot of love for people within themselves, without showing it too openly. This, of course, loosened up with old age, when he stole kisses from my sons, his grandchildren.

That day I saw all the pictures of his grandchildren I had brought for him during the war from their places of exile. They were neatly lined up in the china cupboard in his room. I didn't understand the message he tried to get across with those pictures. But there *was* a message. At the doorstep, he told me: "Zlatko, it's over. My time has come. I will never again see Ogi and Dado, they've destroyed my Old Bridge near the place I grew up, and I can't even hear my violin any more." He had that violin for seventy-three years. The violin itself was more than a hundred and twenty years old. Five years ago, during happier times, he had bequeathed it to his grandson Dražen. He claimed that "the boy most certainly had a good ear for music . . ."

I thought it was a passing thing. He was strong and could still stand on his feet. I didn't realize at the time that no one can stand on their feet if they have had their grandchildren, the very meaning of days to come, taken away from them by force; if the memory of their childhood, as the very meaning of their past, has been taken away from them; and if their violin, as the very sense of the present, has also been taken away. My mother phoned the next morning and couldn't say anything. She cried, and only then did I begin to understand why he had broken his rule the day before by hugging me.

Death by "natural" causes in Sarajevo has a hidden and cruel meaning. My father was not killed by a bullet or a piece of shrapnel intended to damage his body. "They" spared his heart and his head, but they took away something even more precious: they robbed him of past, future, and present.

A day later they "dug him in" at the Lion Cemetery, at "one forty-five." That's what was written on a coffin made out of some kind of thick cardboard. The price—seventy-five marks and five liters of gas. I screamed like crazy at one fifteen, telling them not to start the burial because they said he was "one forty-five," and it was early. I was still waiting for some other friends of his to come, bakers and generals, fishermen, musicians, and journalists . . . Then the gravediggers shouted from further down: "Either you get down here or we'll start filling in. What do we care about time. They kill around here, man."

That's how he was "dug in." A vault bought long ago and now overgrown with weeds, not far from the gaping absence of the Old Bridge, will remain empty forever. The bakers, the generals, the fishermen, and the musicians came at exactly one forty-five, as they had been told. It was too late—for the funeral, for tears, for silence.

Everybody who says that you die in Sarajevo the way you lived is a big liar. In Sarajevo, in fact, life ends only by killing. By "natural" killing and regular killing. After the killing, however, grandchildren stay on to resemble the killed. Grandchildren who are Sarajevans and, only through sheer circumstance, Europeans. And for these grand-children, a violin.